MY
HUSBAND

MY HUSBAND

Maud Ventura

Translated by Emma Ramadan

HUTCHINSON
HEINEMANN

1 3 5 7 9 10 8 6 4 2

Hutchinson Heinemann
20 Vauxhall Bridge Road
London SW1V 2SA

Hutchinson Heinemann is part of the Penguin Random House group of companies
whose addresses can be found at global.penguinrandomhouse.com

Penguin
Random House
UK

First published in the US by HarperVia in 2023
First published in the UK by Hutchinson Heinemann in 2023

Originally published as *Mon mari* in France in 2021 by L'Iconoclaste

www.penguin.co.uk

A CIP catalogue record for this book is available from the British Library.

ISBN (Hardback): 9781529153767
ISBN (Trade paperback): 9781529153774

Designed by Janet Evans Scanlon

Printed and bound in Great Britain by Clays Ltd, Elcograf S.p.A.

The authorised representative in the EEA is Penguin Random House Ireland,
Morrison Chambers, 32 Nassau Street, Dublin D02 YH68

Penguin Random House is committed to a sustainable future
for our business, our readers and our planet. This book is made
from Forest Stewardship Council® certified paper.

MIX
Paper | Supporting
responsible forestry
FSC
www.fsc.org   FSC® C018179

To my parents
love, always

I've never written, though I thought I wrote,
never loved, though I thought I loved,
never done anything but wait
outside the closed door.

The Lover, Marguerite Duras
Translated by Barbara Bray

Prologue

The air is shimmering, the kitchen bathed in sunlight. I hear the shutters opening in the bedroom, the children on the stairs. The house awakens.

My children take their bowls from the cupboard, asking me if I slept well. My husband turns on Brazilian music that pairs perfectly with the smell of toasted bread and the peaceful Sunday morning atmosphere.

While I'm finishing my coffee, my husband leans toward me and whispers into my ear, "We need to find a moment to talk." Then, after a short pause, he adds, "It's important."

I'm frozen, unable to say a word.

It's over.

**Monday,
six days earlier.**

I'm in love with my husband. Or maybe I should say: I'm *still* in love with my husband.

I love my husband as much as the first day I met him. My love hasn't followed a natural progression: the passion from the early days of our relationship never mellowed into tender affection. I think of my husband all the time; I wish I could text him all day. I imagine telling him I love him every morning, and I dream of making love to him every night. But I restrain myself, because I'm too old to act lovesick. Passion is inappropriate with two kids at home, unseemly after so many years of shared life. I know that I have to control myself in order to love.

I don't know of any fictional heroine who can show me how to behave. There are plenty of despairing lovers who sing about loss or rejection. But I don't know of any novel, any film, any poem that can serve as my example, show me how to love better, less intensely.

There is also nothing to appease my anguish, because my husband has already given me everything. I know that we will spend our lives together. I am the mother of his two children. I can't hope for anything more, I can't hope for anything better, and yet the void that I feel is immense, and I am always waiting for him to fill it. But what could possibly fill what is already full?

On Mondays, I never feel even an ounce of fatigue when I walk through the doors to the high school. I've been an English teacher for nearly fifteen years, and I still enjoy my classes. For an hour, I am the center of attention. I am in control; my voice fills the space. I'm also a French–English translator for a publishing house. Maybe this double life is what has kept my passion for teaching intact.

In the teachers' parking lot, I see the principal. We chat for a few minutes. Then comes the moment that I've been waiting for: he asks me how *my husband* is doing. I answer that *my husband* is doing well. Even after thirteen years of marriage, that phrase still has the same effect on me. I tremble with pride when I announce, "*my husband* works in finance," in the teachers' lounge; when I tell my daughter's teacher in front of the school gates, "*my husband* will be picking up the children on Thursday"; when I shop for pastries at the bakery and announce, *"my husband* placed the order on Tuesday"; when I recount in a falsely nonchalant tone (when in reality I find it unbelievably romantic), "I met *my husband* by chance at a rock concert." My husband has no name; he is *my husband*, he belongs to me.

Monday has always been my favorite day of the week. Sometimes it wears a deep royal blue—navy blue, midnight blue, Egyptian blue, sapphire blue. But more often Monday takes on a practical blue, economical and inspirational: the color of Bic pens, my students' workbooks, and simple clothing that goes with everything. Monday is also the day of labels, resolutions, storage boxes. The day of smart choices and reasonable decisions. People have told me that loving Mondays is a brainiac thing—that only nerds are happy when the weekend is over. That might be true. But it comes back to my love of beginnings. I've always preferred the first chapters of a book, the first fifteen minutes of a film, the first act of a play. I like starting points. When everyone is in their rightful place in a world that makes sense.

Late in the morning, I read a text aloud to my students. Then I have them take turns reading. I write down vocabulary on the board, supplying them with the words they need. This position of power is exhilarating. In the piece we're reading today, one of the characters has the same name as my husband. My heart skips a beat each time I see it or when one of my students says it aloud. Then we translate and discuss a couple's exchange of vows. My students are familiar with this Anglo-Saxon tradition, because it's often shown on American TV shows (and often interrupted by an ex-lover trying to win someone back). It's an opportunity to practice the use of the auxiliary verb, thanks to the much-wished-for answer of "I do."

As the last students leave the room, I open the windows to banish the end-of-class odor, a mix of sweat and whiteboard markers, of perfume that is overly sweet (on the girls) and overly musky (on the boys). Teenage hormones go wild for the super-concentrated fragrances they sell in drugstores. Maybe that's the kind of perfume I should buy. For months now I've been wearing a scent from a little-known perfumer that I'd hoped would be sensual but turned out to be hopelessly bland on my skin. How do you know which perfumes are trendy when you're sixteen? I could come up with an exercise on the topic of scents and ask my students to describe their perfume—instructive both for me (so I can pick out a new fragrance) and for them (to enrich their olfactory vocabulary).

Rosa came by while I was at school. I've arranged things so that we don't cross paths, because I never know what to say to her. I haven't lived a wealthy lifestyle for long enough to know how to speak to my cleaning lady—watching her clean my house has always seemed unnatural to me.

In the air is a mild odor of cleanliness; there are damp towels smelling strongly of detergent in the bathroom, and clean linen sheets that have softened over time on our beds. No trace of fingerprints on the large entryway mirror. The red tile floor in the kitchen sparkles.

The figurines on the mantelpiece, the wool blanket on the sofa, the embroidered cushions, the candles on the shelf, the books in the library, the art magazines piled on the coffee table, the framed photos hung in the stair-well: everything is in its place. Even the flowers from the market preside at the center of the dining table with greater poise than before. I'm sure Rosa has rearranged a few stems and leaves to better show off the bouquet.

Yesterday afternoon, my husband went grocery shopping. I'm touched by the abundance in our kitchen: brioche and jam on the counter, our fruit basket filled with apricots and peaches. I know it's silly, but the more my husband runs important errands, the more I feel he loves me. It's as though he's investing in our relationship. Like the green-grocer who weighs the small paper sachets one by one, I can quantify his love each Sunday upon his return from the market depending on the total printed on the receipt in the bottom of the shopping bag. For the fridge: vegetables and meat, tapenade from the olive seller, a salad with grapefruit and crab from the gourmet market, a sizable block of cheese. Seeing this kitchen ready to burst makes my heart skip a beat.

2:30 p.m. It's a bit early to check the mail, but there's no harm in going anyway. Grabbing the key that I keep hidden under the false bottom of my jewelry box, I cross the driveway and open the mailbox with a knot in my stomach. I am relieved to find three letters that have nothing concerning or unusual about them (no handwritten letter or envelope without a stamp). When I look up, I realize that a neighbor is watching me from a few meters away. Panicked, I greet him before rushing back inside.

It's in these moments that I'm most likely to make a mistake, so I take a minute to gather my composure. I put the key back in the false bottom of my jewelry box next to a ring that's still shiny, even though it has oxidized slightly over time. It's nearly twenty years old, but I keep it out of nostalgia, despite the risk: What if my husband found it one day? How would I explain to him why I have a solitaire diamond that's practically identical to the one he gave me the day he proposed?

But my life before doesn't concern him. I don't have to tell him everything: the couples that last are the ones that keep the mystery alive. For example, a few months after we met, I ended things with him. A two-week hiatus during which I ran back into the arms of a former lover, Adrien. We took the train and went to see the ocean. Then, one morning, I left a note on the pillow and I returned to the man who would become my husband. What happened during those two weeks of wavering is none of his business.

Like every Monday, my husband goes to the pool after work. And like every Monday, I cook more nervously than on other nights. I'm agitated, I'm impatient with the children, I cut myself preparing the meal, I overcook the meat.

When my husband is absent, the house resounds less, like a piano whose soft pedal is engaged: the sound comes out muted, domestic life loses variation and intensity. It's as though someone's placed an enormous lid over our roof.

I turn on the porch light, then the lights in the kitchen and the living room. From the street, our house looks like a gift shop glowing in the darkness. It's just the welcoming sight that I want my husband to find upon his return.

Once the children are in bed, I watch TV for a few minutes, but all I see is women who are waiting, just like me. They are eating yogurt, driving a car, or spritzing themselves with perfume, but what sticks out to me is what's happening out of frame: they are all waiting for a man. They're smiling, they seem active and busy, but in reality they are just killing time. I wonder whether I'm the only one to notice the universal women's waiting room.

It's time. My husband will be home any minute. I go to the library looking for a novel to create a certain look. I don't want him to find me waiting in front of a screen. Marguerite Duras will be perfect for tonight.

I read *The Lover* for the first time when I was fifteen and a half. I remember only a few images: the humidity, the sweat, the fluids, the blinds, the Mekong, a girl my age I didn't identify with at all (too detached, too negative). Whether at fifteen or at forty, for me, sex without emotion has never been appealing. Even so, one phrase from the book has always stayed with me: "I've never done anything but wait outside the closed door." I had a funny feeling that I'd already read it somewhere. First I underlined it with a pencil. I had never written on the page of a book before, so this seemed like a very serious gesture. Then, since this still seemed insufficient, I copied the line down in a notebook. At eighteen, I thought about getting it tattooed on my shoulder blade.

Years later, I realized that the phrase wasn't from my past, but from my future. It was not a reminiscence, but a premonition: "I've never done anything but wait outside the closed door."

Legs carelessly folded beneath me, a cup of hot tea within reach, and my book open at random as I am unable to actually read a single line, I await my husband. The living room light is too aggressive. I turn on a lamp, light two candles, and quickly resume my position. From my spot on the sofa, I can see the door reflected in the large entryway mirror. I keep watch for the moment the doorknob finally turns.

It's a common event, a husband returning from work. It happens so often that people stop noticing it. Their focus is on other things: increasingly late hours with each promotion, a meal they don't want to ruin, the children who need to be tucked in. They get used to it, and their attention drifts elsewhere. But I continue to prepare for it each night. I've never stopped noticing.

9:20 p.m. I check my pulse in the hollow of my wrist. Accelerating heart rate, rising blood pressure, state of alarm. A glance in the mirror: my pupils are dilated. I can almost feel the adrenaline spreading through my amygdala; I can almost feel it pulsing, that little almond in my skull, pulsing and spreading its stress signals. I take several deep breaths to try to calm down.

9:25 p.m. I am ready, alert. I run my hand through my hair—my blowout is perfect. I feel the powder on my face, the subtle pink blush on my cheeks. Tonight, I am divine, and I know it: beautiful, but relaxed; beautiful, but seemingly effortless. Discreet but elegant makeup, tight dark jeans and a loose-fitting pale blue blouse. A blouse with buttons to entice my husband to unbutton it. To reveal my lace lingerie, run his hand over my chest, slide my jeans down my thighs, lie me down on the sofa. I want him to dote on me, to take his time, a long time, to spare no effort. Who wouldn't want to do such things to me? I wait, I hope, and my heart races.

9:30 p.m. My husband is on time. His car headlights illuminate sections of the house, announcing his arrival. The car door slams in the street (the first real sign of his return). The mailbox opens and closes with a metallic clang (second sign). Finally, the sound of the key in the lock (final sign, the third knock on the theater stage before the curtain rises). 3, 2, 1. My inner monologue quiets down. All that remains is the uncontrollable beating of my heart. The front door opens. Let the night begin.

Tuesday.

Fifteen years ago, when I noticed that the man with whom I'd just spent the night slept like me, with his hand near his face and wrist bent at a right angle, I wondered how to interpret such a coincidence. Was it the manifestation of a personality trait we had in common? Can people who sleep with their wrist at a right angle identify each other? They say that those who sleep on their backs are sociable, those who lie on their stomachs are sexually frustrated, those who prop themselves on their sides are confident. But they don't say anything about those who sleep with their wrists bent: do we, too, share a commonality? Fifteen years after that first night, I continue to wonder about it.

It's still early when a ray of sun settles itself at the crease of his armpit, making him look like a painting with an expert play of light and shadow. Caravaggio couldn't have found a better model than my husband, with his long black eyelashes at the top of his cheeks and the dampness in the crook of his neck. But it is his body heat in the early morning that has always overwhelmed me more than anything else. (How high can the ambient temperature rise under a down duvet? The microclimate of our bed sometimes seems to approach 50 degrees Celsius after the eight hours spent together under the covers, but is that physically possible?) And then there's his smile. During the night, it's like my husband is on the verge of bursting into laughter, as though someone were telling him a hilarious story between two dreams. This characteristic, one I don't think we share, must be a good sign. An unhappy man doesn't smile in his sleep.

I move my hand close to his head, but stop before my fingers brush his hair. On the pillow is a fine trail of dandruff, like the first snowfall. Often I am moved to find these flakes in our bed or on the collar of a shirt. Is it bizarre to feel tenderness toward my husband's dandruff? I imagine that love is fed by such traces left on a piece of clothing or on a sheet, and that all the lovers of the world are affected by them.

My husband stays asleep until his alarm goes off, even though I opened the bedroom shutters a little while ago now. For years he's insisted that he can sleep only in complete darkness. But I've always preferred to sleep with the shutters open. The dark hours disorient me more than they restore me. My preference doesn't hold much weight compared with my husband's need for darkness. So when we started to share a bed, that concession happened naturally. It's not a big deal in the end. But this morning makes it clear that my husband has been lying to me: obviously, he has no problem sleeping in the light.

As he emerges gently from his sleep, my husband moves closer to me, but I turn around in time to escape his grasp. That's the rule. Last night, he went to sleep without wishing me good night, so he doesn't get any cuddles from me now. It is out of the question for me to give in. Especially on a Tuesday.

Tuesday is a quarrelsome day. The explanation is simple: its color is black and its Latin etymology reveals that it's the day of Mars, the god of war. The storming of the Bastille took place on a Tuesday. September 11, too. Tuesday is always a dangerous day—which is all the more worrying because we have a dinner tonight that I have no desire to attend, and everyone knows that social gatherings are rarely peaceful.

This morning, I immediately recognize from the shower's tepidness that my husband was the last person to use it. I like my showers hotter than him, but I enjoy rinsing with this water chosen by him, in a world a few degrees cooler than my own.

As I wrap myself in my towel, a draft makes me shiver. I apply oil to my hair and lotion to my legs, then a bit of perfume to the hollow of my neck. But upon contact with my skin, the hypnotic aroma transforms into a light, floral fragrance. I bought this perfume after smelling it on another woman at an event. Even through the odor of cigarettes and wine, it immediately evoked a powerful love potion—an enchanting and extremely sensual fragrance. I slipped into our host's bathroom to find out the name of this dangerous poison, and took a photo of the beveled flask (a small, exorbitantly priced perfumer). Alas, from the first spritz, the terrible truth: on my skin, this perfume isn't sexy at all. I've never managed to rid myself of my particular, comforting smell. For years my husband has called me "sweetheart" while I yearn to be a femme fatale.

The smell of coffee and hot chocolate emanates from downstairs. In the kitchen, my husband juices an orange. On the radio, commentators file through the studio. I drink my first cup of coffee during the news roundup: I'm on time.

The children join us at the table for breakfast. My son and my daughter always appear at the same time. Do they plan it before coming down? I watch them systematically disappear together after their meals to go do their homework or play. They're separated by two years—seven and nine—but they could be twins: they do everything together. Our friends and family envy us: *"You're so lucky* your children get along so well, mine barely speak to each other." Actually, our children more than get along: they are co-dependent. (Is this a character trait I passed down to them unwittingly?)

Like every morning, my husband toasts two pieces of bread and covers them in strawberry jam. That's the only one he eats. He won't touch fig, blackberry, or cherry jam—not even a mix of red fruits. This monotheism has always amazed me because my husband doesn't even like strawberries. He finds them too acidic. Only when the small, colorful, juicy fruits are mashed to a pulp and combined with a load of sugar can he appreciate them.

To each his own obsessions. For me, it's my cell phone. I've promised myself a hundred times I will stop putting it on the table during meals; I know it's not healthy, but I can't help it. Fortunately, so far, my husband doesn't seem bothered by it.

He tells me to have a good day and gives me a perfunctory peck. To me, it hardly even counts as a kiss.

In our residential suburb, cars leave and come back with the regularity of the tides: a wave of departures at 8:00 a.m., a wave of returns around 8:30 p.m. (just like with the sea, 12 hours and 25 minutes makes a complete cycle). I am one of the few people out of step with this rhythm, with my part-time teaching and the translation I do from home. From my desk, I watch people come and go.

We live thirty minutes from downtown, in a neighborhood with houses from the 1930s and well-maintained yards that are shielded from view and probably have fruit trees and swings beyond the immense gates. During my childhood, this type of area was an inaccessible dream that came within reach only on Wednesdays when I left my apartment block to go play with my friends in their houses.

Today, I live in the most beautiful house in the neighborhood. Objectively, our façade has the most charm and our trees produce the most fruit. (I read in a decorating magazine that trees give a place its character.) I like its millstones, its lucky green shutters, its mailbox, its flowery driveway, the climbing roses that frame the doorway. (I read in the same magazine that the plant's white flowers are enough to perfume an entire garden on their own.)

On the inside, I like the creaking parquet, the squeaking staircase, the second floor with the master bedroom and the bathroom, the third floor with the children's rooms and my office: the ideal layout.

But my favorite part, hands down, is the entryway. Every night, there is a grand homecoming ceremony: my husband opens the door, sets down the mail (he always insists on getting it), hands me the baguette, drops his keys, and kisses me on the forehead or on the cheek (rarely on the mouth). Such an important scene requires the nicest decor. And so I designed the space with care: a carved mirror that cost a fortune, a beautiful ceramic bowl for our keys, our framed family photos one above the other. It's the first room my husband encounters upon his arrival, so naturally I've paid special attention to it. Otherwise, I will have only myself to blame if my husband stops wanting to come home one day.

The entryway leads to the other rooms on the ground floor: a narrow living room and a minuscule kitchen that looks out onto the garden. I'm not a fan of large, open spaces—they oppress me. I'm more comfortable in these quirky spaces, for which I had custom furniture made. I kept the art deco marble chimney and the ceiling moldings with their complicated garlands. I look at them often when I'm lying on the sofa, wondering whether someone in my family might have made them; my great-grandfather and grandfather were housepainters, and I learned a few years ago that they specialized in plaster moldings.

We moved into this house a few months before I began working as a translator. A colleague from the high school asked me to do a translation of a text for him that he couldn't finish in time—a popular science book on the Copernican Revolution. It was not my area of expertise—I knew very little about the historical period—but I accepted. Since then, the editor has sent me numerous translation projects: stories, a poetry collection, a crime novel that sold fairly well, books on the history of science.

Right now, I'm tackling the debut novel of a success-ful young Irish author. It's not particularly difficult to translate, but the title still escapes me: *Waiting for the Day to Come . . . En attendant que le jour arrive? Dans l'attente du jour à venir?* It resists translation. I can't manage to re-create its poetry, nor capture the concrete meaning. The heroine is not only awaiting the arrival of a new age, of a shift in mentalities. She is also waiting for the literal sun to rise. She must traverse the night and hang on until dawn. Only the first rays of sunlight will secure her salvation. Also, there's an impatience to it that I can't manage to render—an imminence, even. When you read it, it's clear that the day is just about to arrive. *Waiting for the Day to Come* . . . And what to do about the ellipsis?

The rest of the novel hasn't posed any major difficulties. I went about it as usual. I began by familiarizing myself with the structure of the author's thinking. I learned the expressions she prefers, the ways she likes to begin her sentences, the repetitions she can't manage to suppress, her favorite turns of phrase. I entered into her mind and adopted her logic until the mechanics of the whole were revealed to me. After several months of work, I can now say that I have appropriated her expressions and can write in her voice.

At this stage I can savor all the subtleties of her language, which is not very technical, but quite emotive. English is simplistic: no declensions to memorize, no adjective agreement. However, it's a hilly language, irregular and changing: a rudimentary grammar, but expressions that sound good to the ear and an accent impossible to imitate. You can eliminate the syntax errors, expand your vocabulary, adopt the tics of the language, but English will always have a leg up on you. Sometimes I ask myself why I didn't choose a logical, predictable language like German. With English I have to give up all control, which often irritates or frustrates me, but maybe it also explains why I haven't grown tired of it.

People have asked me if my work as a translator has made me want to write my own things. My response has always been the same: I don't think of myself as an author. When I translate, I am merely an interpreter, and that suits me perfectly. I don't have to invent anything, which works out well because I don't have much imagination. I prefer to observe, analyze, deduce; to dissect a text, discover its underlying meanings, uncover its implicit tone—to be on the lookout, like an investigator on the hunt for hidden clues. I also often think back to Marguerite Duras: "I've never written, though I thought I wrote." The second clause in my favorite quotation has always carried that warning: be careful, you're not writing, you're translating.

The smell of the rain-soaked lawn reaches my window. I wish it would never stop raining. My husband is at the office, the children at school; I can continue my work without being disturbed. When my husband is at home, I lose all ability to concentrate. I jump at the slightest sound in the stairwell. As soon as I hear him approaching, I take off my glasses and turn off my computer. I would always prefer that he find me plunged into a thick linguistics textbook or absorbed by the translation of an obscure Byron poem than filling out my students' report cards on the school website. As a precaution, I always have a fountain pen next to me in case my husband enters my office: he loves to see me writing by hand.

He has always admired how rigorously I note the words I need for my translations in my small notebooks. I have a dozen of them. The red notebook is for terms related to politics and societal debates, the blue one is for terms related to nature and the environment. (That one's been written in the most; in particular it contains the names of climbing plants in English gardens and the different species of oak trees). They are all placed side by side on the shelf above my desk, but today I notice that one of them has disappeared. I look everywhere for my yellow notebook, which contains vocabulary related to medicine and the history of the sciences, in vain.

I also have a notebook dedicated to romantic vocabulary, with words that pertain to meeting someone, relationships, separations, and every variation of feeling. Certain recurring expressions give shape to the romantic imagination of the English language—and, by extension, to that of the Irish novelist. (There's no way to prove it, but it seems to me that she blames herself for the devastating loss of her first love, and believes she must pay the price of her past mistakes for her entire life.) For example, the phrase "let you go" is everywhere in her book. "Let you go" is in the mouth of every character and used in every situation: I shouldn't have *let you go*, I will never *let you go*, don't *let me go*, etc. The expression is often used as a form of regret: I'm angry at myself for having let you go, I should have made you stay. We think it's our fault if the other person leaves us, that we could have done something to stop it. We imagine that we could have acted in such a way as to preserve their desire to be together. The idea behind "let you go" is pleasant; there's even something reassuring about it. It's a fiction that I, too, would like to believe in. Absorbed in my translation, I wonder if that expression, so difficult to translate into French, testifies to the fact that English-speakers love differently than us. Do they make more effort? For them, is it possible to make love last? To reignite a desire that's been extinguished? How do they do it? What tender song, new outfit, irresistible perfume, or vacation to the other ends of the earth allows them to hold on to someone on the verge of leaving?

Will "let you go" one day seep into my marriage? How can we protect ourselves from this English blight? Unsurprisingly, even when focused on my translation work, I'm thinking about my husband with each page. All the books I read are about him. During my first translation on the Copernican Revolution (what a scandal: we are not the center of the world, the Earth revolves around the Sun, exiled in an infinite universe), I couldn't stop comparing that scientific discovery with my emotional life. I realized, overwhelmed, that this collapse of all previous points of reference, of everything that had been taken for granted, is exactly what it would feel like if I had to live without my husband. The narrative can unfurl in a distant epoch or in a remote universe: I will still be brought back to him through a description, a love scene, a word. A work on gardening or a book on ancient Egypt can still easily remind me of my husband.

I grab the largest book in our library, pulling the letter from between its pages and placing it on my desk. The envelope has not been opened; I check every Tuesday. In the last few months, I've hidden it in the dresser drawer, in a shoebox, in the wicker basket under my bedside table—but my husband has never found it.

The rain stops. It, too, has abandoned me. I make a cup of tea and sit in the living room armchair—in this spot at this time of day, the light is ideal for reading. I open *The Lover*, which I left out conspicuously on the coffee table. Will my husband notice it this time? Will he pick up on the clues I sprinkle in his path? Last night I was incapable of reading a single line, but this time I lose myself in the novel, which makes my afternoon go by more quickly, effortlessly consuming the remaining hours.

I remind Zoé of the instructions she knows already. It isn't her first time looking after the children: no screens, no tantrums, thirty minutes of mandatory reading before bed. As always, we'll be home before 12:30 a.m. (Having a babysitter waiting at home is a good excuse to cut a dinner short when I'm ready to leave, which will probably be the case tonight.) When it's time to go, I can't stop myself from asking:

"Zoé, be honest. This lamp isn't right, is it?"

Zoé looks at me without saying anything. I don't know if she's afraid of angering me or if she just has no opinion about it. (I myself have spent years developing my refined taste for interior design.) I move the lamp around the sofa, then I try to orient it differently, asking Zoé each time whether it blends better with the space that way.

The lamp is modern and pretty, but the problem is its

intensity. It shines as brightly as a floodlight on a movie set. I'll never be able to make it work; it's impossible to create an intimate, muted ambience with such lighting. I offer it to Zoé. She mumbles that she likes the lamp, but that it wouldn't fit in her small attic room.

How to get rid of it? Lost in thought, I leave without kissing my children goodbye. I said a few words to them in the stairwell before shutting the door, asked them to behave and listen to Zoé, but I forgot to embrace them. I tell myself that it's no big deal, I shouldn't make a big thing of it. Does this happen to other mothers? Do they also forget to kiss their children's cheeks before leaving the house? At what age do they drop the physical affection with every goodbye? My children are seven and nine. Does that mean they can finally do without my hugs? I wonder whether Zoé will think I'm a bad mother.

My friends often ask me where I get my hair done, but I never tell them. I stumbled upon the salon by chance back in the days when I would change hair-stylists after every cut. At the time, I had developed a bad habit of inventing a personality for myself over the course of a dye job or a nail appointment; it was a way to escape my daily life once per month, with no consequence and at little cost. That particular time, I'd said my name was Grace. I had chosen my favorite Hitchcock blond, Grace Kelly: glacial but sensual, sophisticated but savage. My choice was not exactly random; a few years earlier, in college, I had dedicated my final essay to that hair color and its role in the famous director's films. That winter, I had gone into the salon with the firm intention of transforming myself into Grace for a few hours. Childish, but thrilling. I explained that I had just gotten married after a rapid divorce. A passionate reunion with my childhood sweetheart, an American photographer I'd lost touch with for years and ran into again by chance at a gallery opening. Drawn like a magnet to one of the portraits on the wall, I had approached it and found his name on the mat at the bottom of the frame. By the time I realized it was my former lover, he was standing behind me. I am not proud of this lie, but I assumed I would never go back to that salon.

As it happened, that hairdresser gave me the most beautiful color I've ever had. In the following weeks, I received a shower of compliments about my blond hair, cold and sensual at the same time—and although I continued to deny that it wasn't my natural color, I admitted to my friends that I do get a balayage from time to time. I tried other salons, without ever managing to achieve that same color. Maybe it was Grace alone who succeeded in inspiring this lethal, icy blond in my colorist (even though she wasn't familiar with Hitchcock's films— I asked her). So I had no choice but to return. Now I transform into Grace once a month to maintain my blond and get my nails done impeccably. I recount my romantic escapades with my second husband, his latest exhibitions in New York. And my occasional sadness at not being able to have children.

Today, I ask for a color that's slightly warmer than usual—I want to brighten things up ahead of summer.

But it's important that the change not be too abrupt. I don't want my husband to notice, and a blond that doesn't appear natural can easily seem vulgar. She doesn't change the length: I never cut off more than necessary because my husband prefers me with long hair. He loathes in-betweens, in life and in my hair. I buy several overpriced hair products that I'll hide in our closet, with my other chamomile lightening sprays. Finally, I choose a pale pink for my nails. It's less sophisticated than an intense red, but I've seen several mothers picking up their children from school and at the tennis club with this color.

When I leave the salon, my husband has only just left work, and we decide to meet directly at our friends' house. Nicolas and Louise are the proud parents of a little three-month-old girl whom we will finally meet for the first time.

I stop in a store downtown to find a gift for the baby. I choose a soft stuffed whale that also serves as a pajama pouch. I had something similar when I was little, where I stashed my treasures. And what more beautiful gift is there than a hiding place? I also bring an illustrated children's book I found at an Anglophone bookstore last weekend: it's about adventure, with landscapes from all over the world, snowy mountains and infinite oceans, a canoe drifting on a raging stream, a hot-air balloon flying over a sandy desert. Perfect for a little girl.

My last stop is at the florist. Of course, I've done my research before arriving. Typing in the search engine, "What kind of flowers do you give for the birth of a child," I learned that I should bring white flowers—peonies or roses, for example. I tried to figure out which were the most chic (I suspect roses are a bit more common and the peonies more distinguished), but couldn't find a definitive answer.

I hate asking for advice at the florist. I refuse to reveal that I know nothing, that I can't tell the difference between a violet and a pansy, that I would be incapable of picking out a daffodil, an iris, or a hyacinth. I prefer to do my research ahead of time. Women are supposed to know this kind of thing. Louise would never have needed advice to choose a bouquet. She would have wandered around the store with a smile, stopping from time to time to smell a flower, then turned to the salesclerk and declared: "You have a very beautiful store." At one point, she would have stopped short, surprised and enthralled: "Oh, you have honeysuckle again, how marvelous! The smell reminds me of my childhood! I'll take a few— maybe with two or three roses!" But I didn't grow up in a house where honeysuckle bouquets infused the living room. So I say as little as possible. The secret is not asking any questions. I don't ask how often to change the water or if I should cut the end of the stems once back at home.

My manicured fingers, my shiny hair, and the imposing diamond on my ring finger imbue me with the courage necessary to finally address the salesclerk. To give myself an air of importance, I even let slip that I'm in a rush (which isn't true), pause at the lilies, then ask for a bouquet of peonies. I find the lilies quite beautiful, but I don't know enough about them: they are indeed white, but what if they're condolence flowers? Pink and white peonies, which conform to the advice of the site I consulted earlier, are a safer bet.

As the florist prepares the bouquet, she announces:

"It's wedding season! Everyone wants peonies! They make such beautiful bouquets. It's really one of my favorite flowers," she adds with a look of concentration as she snips expertly with her scissors.

I crumple.

"It's not for a wedding . . . It's for a friend who's just had a baby . . ." I stammer, tears in my eyes. I've chosen the wrong flowers. I must have confused peonies and daisies.

The florist looks up at me with large green eyes and smiles kindly.

"Peonies also make for a very beautiful baby gift. These are flowers for happy occasions, they'll be perfect for your friend! Don't worry."

I rush to pay, humiliated. In my hands, the bouquet seems much too large, like the bouquet of a young bride in a frilly princess dress. It's no match for Louise's elegance. Overly imposing bouquets are not at all refined—I realize that now. I consider throwing a few flowers in the trash to render it slightly more delicate and a bit less *young girl in flower*. But when I turn the corner of the street, my husband is already waiting for me in front of the building.

"Did you do something to your hair?" he asks me with a quick kiss. (When will he finally really kiss me? Anything less than two seconds is not the kiss of someone in love.) I avoid his question, but he insists:

"Your dress is beautiful, is it new? You look incredible, sweetheart."

Uneasy, I change the subject as I search for our friends' names on the intercom.

When we arrive, their apartment is slightly messier than usual. We glimpse their little Violette asleep in her crib. My husband and I find ourselves opposite two young parents as exhausted as they are radiant.

Nicolas and Louise live in an impressive apartment that we would never be able to afford. My husband greatly envies his childhood friend, but I don't. I prefer our house. I prefer our life. Nicolas had many relationships and partners before meeting Louise, he married for the first time last year, he earns a lot of money thanks to a high-ranking finance job, he travels often and far away, he goes to see trendy plays, he dines in fancy new restaurants that we've never heard of. In a word, Nicolas is free, and that means that he lives in a modern duplex downtown while my husband lives in a bourgeois house in the suburbs. And for that, my husband still resents me a bit.

Louise thanks me for the flowers. I follow her through the apartment while she searches for a vase. The first she finds is too small. I apologize, ashamed. Louise laughs and thanks me again for "the very beautiful bouquet," but I think I sense a hint of irony in her voice. She places the peonies on a side table in the living room. Amid the modern and minimalist decorations, this huge pastel bouquet seems ridiculous.

Louise looks sublime in her long black dress, and I can't stop myself from commenting that the color of the dress and her haircut suit her well. I'm mad at myself as soon as the words come out of my mouth. It's a habit I've been trying to correct for years: I can't help complimenting a necklace, an outfit, a lipstick, or a perfume I like. I need to settle for discreetly finding out where they come from and buying them later instead. I've always admired the women around me too much, and revealing this to them renders me insidiously inferior in comparison. I must learn to restrain myself. To do it less. Louise thanks me, but does not return the compliment. In bourgeois milieus, people rarely compliment each other.

I reassure myself by methodically reminding myself of all the reasons I don't need to worry: my nails are impeccable, my hair is perfect, my outfit is elegant. I know because I only buy clothing that I've seen worn by women with irreproachable style, or in unquestionably trustworthy stores. The new dress I'm wearing tonight is no exception: black and white, silk, deceptively simple and sensible, perfectly cut, spotted this season at a cocktail party. When it comes to clothes, I prefer not to take any risks, and I pay whatever the price is without batting an eye. I breathe and gently tap two fingers on the inside of my wrist to restore my calm (a technique that a sophrologist taught me to slow my heart rate) while reciting comforting mantras to myself: *No one can see my neuroses except me. The way I see myself is not how other people see me. Everything is okay. I belong here.*

And besides, I have my beauty going for me. That I've never doubted. Objectively, I am prettier than Louise. I scrutinize her faults with a glance: I am taller and thinner than her, my features more delicate. When she moves gracefully through her large immaculate apartment and her dress flutters with each of her movements, yes, you might think that Louise is pretty. But if you approach her to get a closer look, you notice rather quickly that her face is not as graceful (her nose, above all), and that she's a few pounds overweight (that was already the case and her pregnancy did her no favors). Her apparent beauty would not withstand a less sophisticated outfit or an apartment in the suburbs with questionable decor. Louise is not a true beauty: she pays to be pretty.

That's not the case for me. My parents may not have

left me anything else, but at least they had the courtesy to pass down good genes. People have been complimenting me on my appearance since I was a child. As a teenager, when I was at the mall in my working-class neighborhood with no makeup on, in jeans and an old pair of sneakers, people would do double takes. Apparently I already resembled Nicole Kidman—something about my eyes, people told me often. Something in my coldness, too, I imagine.

Thanks to my husband, I have fine-tuned my beauty. I can now afford to make myself look the way I always wanted to, leaving my lower-class self behind. I maintain my sculpted body with yoga and tennis. I learned elegance (which in the end comes down to three things: an overpriced coat, purse, and shoes. Once this holy trinity has been achieved, the rest is easy). I know now that a lady must not place her handbag on the ground while eating on a restaurant terrace, but on her knees or on the chair next to her. I take my delicate clothing to the dry cleaner. I have my shoes polished every season. I've learned how to apply discreet but stylish makeup (one must never seem to be wearing makeup—with the exception of a crimson or burgundy lipstick). I pay to have my nails done. I go to the hairdresser every month so that my roots are never visible. Another revelation I had was that the impeccable hairstyles of the women I once so admired are not the result of a miracle, genetics, or class privilege, but are instead the natural outcome of a daily blowout that requires only two things: a professional hair dryer and the right hairbrush. And that's how I became one of those women with no runs in her tights, how I learned to match my appearance to the bourgeois house my husband and I bought.

"To Violette!"

We are clinking our champagne glasses when my husband says to Nicolas and Louise (in a complicit tone): "Welcome to real life!" I don't know how to interpret this. What does my husband mean? What exactly is real life? We discuss their new status as young forty-something parents, diapers, bottles. Holding his champagne glass, my husband talks about the period when our son wasn't yet sleeping through the night and was crying for hours on end, keeping us awake and feeling powerless. He reassures Nicolas, reminding him that children grow up, that the lack of sleep, the tears, the screams don't last forever. Is that what my husband means to say when he announces so solemnly to his friends that they are entering "real life"? Does he mean an unexciting and overly restrictive existence? Does "real life" for him amount to abandoning his dreams and renouncing his freedom?

So my husband is nursing a painful memory from the months that followed the birth of our son. I think again with emotion of my husband cradling him carefully, his immense hands on the baby's minuscule body, our relief when he finally fell asleep, our nervous and conspiratorial laughter the next morning even though we had slept only a few hours ourselves. These memories with my husband are all the more precious because the three of us lived essentially in isolation during that period. We couldn't have visitors or leave our house because our son, born prematurely, had a compromised immune system. It turned out to be a blessing for our relationship.

Before moving to the table, Nicolas and Louise show us the first photos of Violette, thoughtfully arranged in an album with a brief caption and a date at the bottom of each page to preserve the memory. Like Louise, I started a photo album when I met my husband, with the places and years written in pen. I never kept albums of photos of my trips or with my friends before him. My husband marks the start of when my life was worth being archived.

"I don't understand why anyone wouldn't breastfeed their child! It makes no sense!" Louise exclaims just before we move to the table.

This candor is what best characterizes her. I'm now used to it, but it still leaves me speechless sometimes.

Louise says things that, from someone else's mouth, could be hurtful. But a profound warmth renders them inoffensive. Her smile disarms her words. I opted not to breastfeed my children, and Louise knows this. But she deems this fact of little importance and therefore there's no reason I should take it the wrong way: she is simply stating her opinion. I remember the day when Louise said to me: "I absolutely hate the color green! It reminds me of my mother!" while I was wearing a green dress—and she saw no problem with doing so.

Louise is whimsical, loud, and frank, while Nicolas is elegant, restrained, and thoughtful. (Tonight, they are both being precisely themselves.) Nicolas is one of those people who makes the effort to step into your universe. His questions show that he's interested in my life, that he thinks of me even when we haven't seen each other for a while. He asks me how my work is going with my editor, how my classes are going, if I've read that series by a New York novelist he's just started, what I think of the translation.

Nicolas is as reserved as Louise is sociable. Louise is as indelicate and brusque as Nicolas is considerate and attentive. She is radiant. He tempers her. Together, they complement each other, like two pieces of machinery that fit together exactly, a perfectly oiled gear where the deviations are also the synergies that render movement possible. I believe this is what we call "chemistry."

The table is quickly covered in dishes, bread, wine. The meal is excellent. I appreciate the dinner all the more because I loathe having people over. I never know what to prepare; it takes me weeks to decide. Fortunately my husband takes charge of picking out the wine, which I am completely incapable of doing. I could buy the most expensive bottle at the wineshop, but there's a risk of seeming ridiculous: you wouldn't bring a wine that costs hundreds of euros to a casual barbecue. I've been afraid of people thinking I have bad taste ever since I realized my husband's money wouldn't buy me elegance or good manners.

My hands are always visible (never on my knees). I pass dishes to the left. I wait for Louise to offer before I serve myself more fish. I let Nicolas refill my wineglass. I don't take more cheese. When the meal ends, my silverware is parallel on the plate and my napkin placed on the table, and I've taken care not to refold it. I know these rules now, but I had to make an effort to learn them. I've been practicing for fifteen years. I can even perform them with a semblance of effortlessness now.

When I met my husband's family, I felt that there were certain codes I hadn't mastered, but I couldn't yet identify them. One day, I witnessed a troubling scene. My husband's older sister, mother to a boy of around ten or so, was scolding him, and I didn't grasp what he had done wrong until much later. First there was a warning for a laugh that was slightly too loud, followed by a reprimand for his elbows being on the table. And then I heard her say: "I'm going to buy you Nadine de Rothschild's book of etiquette if you keep on like this!" I thought it was just an expression, but soon I discovered that this manual actually existed. I bought it a few weeks later and a parallel universe opened up to me. A world in which plates are always passed clockwise.

Holding this book between my hands, I understood that there was a reason for the unease I had felt among my husband's family. It wasn't just my imagination or a lack of self-confidence: I had in fact committed unforgivable errors. I had taken off my shoes upon arrival (I thought I was doing the right thing, that's what my parents had always taught me), and I had served myself a second helping of chocolate as we drank coffee (this was out of gluttony). I had even mopped up my plate with a piece of bread using my hands and not my fork. (I learned later that one should really refrain from mopping up their plate at all.) So in a new notebook I wrote down notes categorized thematically: dinners, gifts, posture. I promised myself that I would learn all of these rules by heart. And Nadine de Rothschild gave me the education that I had never received.

During the meal, Nicolas keeps calling my husband by a childhood nickname that only Nicolas uses. This version of my husband that I don't recognize is unsettling to me. I am even more unsettled when Nicolas tells me something I didn't know about my husband. The idea that Nicolas knew him during a time when I hadn't yet met him makes me slightly dizzy. More generally, the idea that my husband existed before meeting me is surreal, even revolting.

When Louise and Nicolas start to talk about their honeymoon, my entire body tenses. It's a subject I would rather avoid. Louise describes landscapes that interest me very little (is it ever fun to look at other people's vacation photos?) and in the process reminds me of a painful memory I'd rather forget.

My husband had the wonderful idea to get sick during our honeymoon. "How could he do this to me?" I would constantly ask myself whenever I saw his pale face. A flu pinned him to the bed for seven days straight. My husband didn't even have the originality to catch a tropical illness, a local malady with impressive symptoms, something that could have become a funny or dramatic anecdote to tell upon our return. That week, I wandered alone down the hotel hallways. I drank cocktails at the bar and let a married man flirt with me. I told my husband that I joined the hotel's hiking group to explore the island with a guide. In reality, I didn't go on any outings. What was the point of an eight-hour excursion around a volcano if my husband wasn't with me to see it? What good was it to walk along that flat blue ocean if he wasn't walking by my side? Why go to that hot, remote island if I was alone in the photos?

The following Monday, my husband was finally feeling better. We went for walks on all the days that followed and I found the island sublime, with the most beautiful landscapes I had ever seen. But still today, as soon as the topic of our honeymoon comes up, I feel a sharp bitterness toward my husband, who ruined half of that magical vacation for me. An idyllic honeymoon might have given me the strength necessary to confront the first months of our marriage.

Just before dessert, we talk about my husband's birthday party three months ago (finally, a topic of conversation that is a priori inoffensive). The four of us agree that the party was a success. Then my husband recounts what happened at the end of the night after Nicolas and Louise had left to go back to their baby: the electricity went out and the room was plunged into silence and darkness. The guests started to sing, and then the security alarm went off due to the power outage.

"Fortunately, thanks to my phone flashlight, I quickly found the alarm panel, and I even guessed the code. I figured it had to be something simple . . . And it was one-two-three-four!"

My husband is a good storyteller. That might even be the main source of his charisma: he recounts stories so well that it's easy to imagine the tipsy guests surprised by the screeching alarm, my husband setting off in search of the panel, guessing the code, taking control of the situation with humor and courage. Nicolas and Louise listen; they are amused, but I am not. My husband has not once uttered my name. I am absent from his story—erased. He says "I," referring only to himself, and it embarrasses me. (I've analyzed enough literary texts in my life to know that it's not innocuous.) It was thanks to the light on *my* phone that we found the panel. It was *me* who suggested to him that a rental space would probably choose a code that's easy to remember. It was *me* who tried 0000, then 1234. Why doesn't he say that? Why doesn't he say I was part of the story, too?

My husband concludes by thanking Nicolas and Louise for contributing to his birthday gift. In fact, he's wearing his new watch tonight. But not a word of thanks to me for having organized the surprise, sent the invitations, reserved the space, paid the security deposit, chosen the watch, washed the fifty champagne flutes at four in the morning.

I listen to Nicolas and Louise: they say *we*. Their grammar is inclusive: if one of the two of them is the main character of the story, the other is never erased because of it—the other's point of view is always included in the narrative ("When I told Louise the next day, she was so surprised!"). I also observe their way of being together. Just looking at them, you can tell there is an equal division of tasks, an equilibrium of their characters, complementary faults. He has a reassuring voice; she has a magnificent laugh. While Nicolas clears the table, Louise serves a final glass of wine. The two of them perform an impeccable choreography, a seamless lovers' ballet. When Louise joins Nicolas in the kitchen, he leans toward her and kisses her on the mouth, his hand on her hip. Catching others in the act of kissing remains one the most fascinating spectacles in the world for me.

A small camera would be easy to hide in their living room. It would only take a moment, while they're both in the kitchen and my husband has gone into one of the bedrooms on a phone call. I could place a tiny recording device above their TV, for example. From there, I would have a view of their sofa.

I wish I could observe them once the guests leave. I'd like to see how they behave once they're finally alone. I wish I could watch their relationship from day to day; I wonder if they still seem so in love when the baby has been crying a lot, when fatigue sets in, when the worries pile up, or when one of them falls ill.

Do they kiss at night on the sofa? Do they make out intensely or simply graze lips? Do they also have nights when they don't kiss with tongues? Do they touch each other nonstop or is there space between their bodies when they watch TV? How much time do they spend talking to each other at night, and what do they talk about? Do they say they love each other every day? Every week? Every month?

Observing them would allow me to compare their relationship with ours. I could determine whether my husband and I kiss a lot or a little, gauge the interest and depth of our daily conversations. Armed with this quantitative and qualitative data, I could thus evaluate whether our relationship is normal or cold.

After dinner, as we are leaning out the windows amid cigarette smoke and the aroma of red wine, we decide to prolong the night with a game. Each player is assigned a fruit that they then have to make their team guess.

My husband chooses the clementine for me. I try not to reveal just how wounded I am. Is he trying to tease me or get a rise out of me? I ask him about it in a lighthearted tone, without insisting. He answers that he doesn't know why he chose this particular fruit, but that it suits me well. And then my husband stands up to serve himself more wine. Is it a coincidence, or is he avoiding confrontation?

I know my husband. I know the sharpness of his gaze. I know his perceptiveness and the precision of his associations of ideas. I know the ease with which he manages to encapsulate a person in one or two phrases. I have to face facts: the man I've been married to for more than ten years thinks of me as a clementine.

For Louise, my husband chooses a pineapple. Right in front of me, he associates his best friend's wife with a summery, exotic fruit, acidic and ample. He associates her with Latin America and implies, I'm convinced, that he is intrigued by the juicy flesh of that tropical plant.

So my husband thinks his best friend is married to a pineapple, while he married a clementine. He lives with a winter fruit, a banal and cheap fruit, a supermarket fruit. A small, ordinary fruit that has none of the indulgence of the orange nor the originality of the grapefruit. A fruit organized into segments, practical and easy to eat, precut, ready for use, proffered in its casing.

Although my husband has had more to drink than I have, I refuse to drive home. I am not in a state to drive; I'm much too aggrieved by the clementine incident. I want an explanation, but I am still much too distraught to confront the issue head-on. Even the white lights of the city through the window cannot soothe me. I don't say a word the whole way home.

We find Zoé asleep on the sofa, the TV projecting disturbing shadows onto her body. She lives in the next town over, and my husband suggests he drive her home. I refuse.

"I'll call you a taxi, Zoé," I reply firmly.

My husband won't get out of this so easily. Evade me by driving Zoé back home so that I'll be asleep when he returns? Much too clever on his part. He's not going anywhere. He's staying with me.

My husband pulls some bills out of his wallet to pay her (this sight has always moved me to an unreasonable degree, but it's not enough to extinguish my anger tonight), then he heads up to bed. Before joining him, I take a few minutes alone to write down the main incidents that occurred this evening: his negative account of the first months with our son, his erasure of me from the story of his birthday party. And above all, the clementine. A line with the fountain pen to record his betrayal, as bitter as the supermarket fruit.

I write regularly in this notebook to reflect on my experiences. It's not a diary in the proper sense. I don't go into detail. Everything can be summed up in a line or two, and then the solution to my anxiety or my anger becomes obvious. It's a funny habit that I've never told anyone about, but writing does me good. I have another notebook that I keep hidden in the same place, behind the library books. A green notebook where I copy down the ideas and advice I read in magazines, where I take notes on articles I read on the Internet.

I put my notebook back in its place, behind a series of encyclopedias. I am still humiliated and furious, but at least I know what to do now. Writing always shows me the solution.

When I join my husband in the bedroom, I open the window as if to enlarge the space between us. I ask him if we can leave the shutters open for once. He refuses. The light and sound from the street keep him from sleeping. And he doesn't understand this sudden questioning of what has come to be established as routine between us for years: we sleep with the shutters closed.

I gave him an opportunity to compensate for the clementine, to prove that he is capable of making an effort, that he isn't opposed to compromise. He did not seize that chance. Too bad for him. I restrain myself from informing him that he continued to sleep this morning even with a ray of sunlight directly on his face. If only I had the courage to challenge him: "I know that isn't true, sweetheart, you were sleeping perfectly well with the shutters open this morning—spare me the absurd lie, it's getting ridiculous."

I am sitting on the edge of the bed and trying to remain completely still when suddenly two tears run down my face and meet beneath my chin. They trace a translucent path in the shape of a heart along my cheeks.

I have learned over the years to identify two different kinds of tears. First, tears of frustration or rage. Violent, severe, red tears. They don't stream, they spurt. It's easy to recognize them because they leave behind puffy faces and swollen eyes. These are tears that come to me when the children are at their grandparents' house during school vacation, dinner is ready, I am ready, and my husband calls me to say that he'll be home late because of an urgent thing at work he has to take care of. Then I hang up and cry tears of rage. I hate getting dressed up for nothing.

And then there are, as is the case tonight, tears of sadness. They also don't stream, they overflow. After several days of continuous, vague sadness, they slide down the face in silence, one after another. These are icy tears, not very abundant, a very light, almost transparent blue. They act as a shield: these protective tears place a damp bandage over the cheek. It's enough to wipe them away with the back of your hand.

I've barely dried my two crystalline tears when I hear my husband's slow breathing. How can he fall asleep so easily after what he's done to me? He puts the energy and determination that I dream of investing in our relationship into his sleep.

While my husband sleeps with revolting ease, I watch our marriage flash before my eyes. In this moment, I am intimately persuaded: it's over. Our relationship is now bereft of love. After fifteen years of life together, I believe I deserve more than being compared with a vulgar clementine. My husband is going to leave me. I can picture it already: signing the divorce papers at one end of the table, my eyes red with tears, moving into a tiny, dark two-bedroom, unable to find another man over forty, nights spent single-handedly taking care of the children I never wanted.

I have to get out of bed. Trembling, I drink a glass of water in the kitchen. I remove my wedding ring and leave it on the entryway table next to the ceramic pot where our keys rest intertwined. I want to get a reaction out of him.

When I finally find a comfortable position in the bed, my entire body starts to itch. The same thing happens every night. Right as I'm about to fall asleep, my body itches: my head, my thighs, my elbows, my neck, my stomach.

I've consulted doctors, a dermatologist, a homeopath. I've tried to treat it as a skin problem and a sweat problem. I've checked for fleas in the bed. I've checked the humidity level in the room. I've changed the detergent a hundred times, thinking I might be allergic to a certain fragrance or ingredient.

My body itches. I try to think about something else. But I am hounded by a single question: Why a clementine? If only I could relive that dinner, listen again to the events of the night in order to understand how he could have come to that conclusion. I know it's a Tuesday, the day of conflict, but a clementine is still a particularly vehement declaration of war.

The minutes pass, but I have no idea what time it is because the closed shutters and drawn curtains keep me from glimpsing the emerging sun. I am both exhausted and unable to sleep. During this time, my husband continues to revel in his egotistical sleep. In this moment, I detest him. There is no other solution: I scream as though I'm having a nightmare. He wakes up with a jump. I stammer in a falsely sleepy voice that I'm sorry, just a bad dream, and turn back to my side of the bed. I hope my husband can't fall back asleep and that his insomnia will leave him the time necessary to reflect on his betrayal. It's important that he ask himself: How could he have reduced his own wife to the rank of a vulgar clementine? Why not a banana?

Wednesday.

I'm in a bad mood. Wednesday is an orange day, like a clementine. Since this morning, I've been taunted by several objects with an orange hue: my mandarin-scented daytime lotion, my watchband, the grated carrots for tonight's dinner in the fridge.

I spent the night ruminating on all the fruits I could think of. I arrived at the following conclusion: I would have liked to be a peach, a blackberry, or a cherry. I hate being a clementine, but I also wouldn't have appreciated being a pear, a banana, or a grape.

"You forgot your ring last night when we came home, it was downstairs next to the keys!" my husband crows, handing me my solitaire diamond ring (a fitting name: I have never felt so alone as I have since I've married him).

His naiveté is unbearable. My husband is so certain of

my love that even my ring placed on the entryway table does not come across as a threat to him. What world is he living in?

Even if the clementine incident hadn't happened, we should never have accepted Nicolas and Louise's invitation. What a pointless dinner. When I'm with my husband, I don't need to see our friends. I also don't have any desire to visit my parents, and I don't miss my children. My husband is enough for me. He, on the other hand, likes to be surrounded by people. He comes alive when he's among groups. He likes going out and meeting new people. But his sociability is painful for me. Each new person who enters into our life is an additional dilution of his attention, a dilution of him, and I'm horrified by this. The energy he expends toward others hurts me: it tells me that I am not enough for him.

If I close my eyes and imagine it, my greatest joy would be a life restricted to the space of our home. My ideal situation would be endless one-on-one time with my husband: the two of us in our living room, drinking strong coffee, talking for hours on end. Sometimes, I picture myself alone on the earth with him. I invent a fatal epidemic, a nuclear war that leaves us the only survivors, or a desert island where we wash up after a plane crash. When I think of my greatest happiness, it's always just the two of us: we are alone and we are together. I can't help it—my paradise is being in a couple, a duo, a pair.

I think back to the way we were at the beginning: before the children, the house, the commute, the daily routine. It was a time when my husband was sweeter, more tender, more affectionate. His hands would be clammy when he came to meet me, and he would do everything in his power to make me happy. Our love lived at a different rhythm; it was nourished each day, always expanding.

He would come to the tiny room I was renting at eleven in the morning or three in the afternoon, whenever I wasn't teaching, to make love to me. He was finishing his studies, and I had just started work: when you're twenty-five you can have sex on a weekday, devote your morning or afternoon to it. I had a twin bed, so I bought a second mattress that I kept under mine. When he came over, we would put the two mattresses on the floor, covering the entire surface area of my top-story, 160-square-foot studio. Those two mattresses pushed together formed our raft: we were alone in the world, in the middle of an imaginary ocean.

When we made love, we'd end up with our heads where our feet should be, the duvet balled up in a corner. I remember that he wouldn't undress me: he would touch me through my clothes until I gave in and removed them myself, one by one. He would touch me over my jeans, then over my underwear. He'd descend gently between my legs to delicately kiss the fabric: a restraint that drove me wild, a modesty that made me delirious. When I close my eyes, I can still feel his breath as he planted a kiss between my thighs, on the thin strip of cotton. He would spend long minutes circumventing my want, dancing around my desire—I would be champing at the bit, raring for something tangible: a finger, a tongue, an ass cheek. He would do everything except what I was dying for him to do. He already understood that desire was born out of frustration, that it is often more effective to suggest than to do. He would keep me unsatisfied, awaiting my liberation. I had never so badly wanted to be penetrated. So I would drown in happiness when he finally thrust into me. And by the time he turned me over on the mattress and lifted my legs, I was already dreaming of my wedding dress. I'd moan to encourage him and think to myself: I'm sure this will be the man to put a ring on my finger, I'm sure he sees me as his wife and the future mother of his children. The proof: he doesn't pull my hair and doesn't ask me to go down on him.

I'm about to leave for school when my husband calls for me. He can't find his wallet and he's going to be late to drop off the kids at school. He doesn't understand why it's not on the entryway table—he was sure he put it there, as he was the one who paid Zoé last night.

"You looked in the pockets of the pants you were wearing yesterday?"

I feel like I've lived out this scene a thousand times: my husband asks me why his wallet or his keys aren't where he thinks he left them. Sometimes it's his cell phone. For years I've been telling him to put his things in the same place, but it's no use. I hear my husband rushing around the bedroom, then silence. I was right: his wallet was in fact in his pants pocket.

His forgetfulness began seemingly overnight a few months after the birth of our daughter. My husband wound up going to see a doctor, unnerved by his suddenly faulty memory. Sometimes he feels like he's going crazy. No problems for weeks, and then a watch disappears from the bathroom, only to show up later in a drawer. Since the scans and the neurological tests revealed nothing (no brain damage, no degenerative illness), we both chose to laugh about it. Ever since, we've been joking about his absent-mindedness: my husband has his head in the clouds! He's so scatterbrained! He forgets everything: his keys, his computer, his cell phone, his charger, the grocery list. Fortunately, he's never left the kids in a supermarket cart or in the car during a heat wave.

Both my hands are on the wheel, but I can't bring myself to start the engine. The unbearable floral odor of my perfume permeates the entire car; I lower the windows, but outside it's the same thing—it smells like a bourgeois garden (it's always a losing battle against jasmine and rose). I glance in the rearview mirror and notice that I put on the wrong scarf. When I reached into the drawer earlier, I grabbed the one with the orange pattern (ever since my husband turned me into a clementine, I've solemnly sworn never to wear clothing of this color again), when I thought I'd grabbed the green one. I didn't realize my mistake because I was getting dressed in the dark.

During the drive, I am hounded by a long procession of orange objects: an advertisement for Sicily orange juice at a red light, and then an orange car stops next to me. I laugh nervously. I hate Wednesdays, and not only because the children don't go to school on Wednesday afternoons and we have to take care of them (don't get me started with football, dance, and music classes we have to take them to). Wednesday is also the day of Mercury. That little chaotic, harried planet governs my sign, Virgo, and I am often at the mercy of its trajectory through the solar system. As soon as it goes into retrograde, as it is now, everything gets complicated: I struggle to communicate, I start questioning everything, I'm highly emotional. I hate Wednesdays and I hate Mercury.

My orange scarf is becoming more and more unbearable. At first it was a slight inconvenience. Then I started having trouble breathing as I crossed the school courtyard. Now, inside the classroom, I'm suffocating. I take it off and throw it out the window. Some students trample on it down below. I can no longer stand having the evidence of my husband's transgression—that of keeping me from opening the shutters—knotted around my neck. It's because of him that I have to get dressed in the dark. And it's because of him that I put on the wrong scarf this morning.

To calm myself down, I repeat what my mother always used to say: *marriage is all about compromise.* Sleeping with the shutters closed, *it's no big deal.* What's more, many couples sleep that way; after all, it's just a question of habit. And scientists agree that sleep is more restorative in complete darkness. So *it's no big deal.* But after fifteen years, can we still say *it's no big deal?* 5,478 nights, is that really so negligible? 5,478 mornings of sleeping slightly worse—doesn't that add up? 5,478 nights of not being woken up by natural light, isn't that a sacrifice that merits my outrage?

Because of those closed shutters, I sleep poorly. And the lack of sleep chips away at my health and increases my risk of cancer. I'm not as efficient as I could be at work and I drive more dangerously on the road. Fifteen years of being more irritable, of having less patience with my children and students, of having a harder time memorizing new information. Fifteen years of bad sleep, a vague fatigue that slows my reaction time: if I were to witness an accident or if the house were to catch fire, the consequences could be disastrous. On top of it, sleeping poorly makes you gain weight, and my husband is the first to compliment me on my slenderness. Those 40,000 hours of destructive sleep in the dark, who will give them back to me? What will compensate for them?

Marriage is all about compromise. But why did I have to be the one to adapt? There was no more reason for it to have been me to give in rather than him. And yet the closed shutters became a foregone conclusion between us. It was hardly a question. My husband could always cover his eyes with a sleep mask, but I can't artificially replicate natural light in our bedroom. Plus, yesterday, when I opened the shutters, the sunlight didn't even wake him up. Is his sleep really as light as he claims? One day he declared that he could sleep only in complete darkness, and that was that. Maybe he wouldn't even notice the difference.

The injustice is so flagrant to me now and so is—I hardly dare say it—the lie. Has my husband tricked me into believing that he can't sleep with the shutters closed when in reality he has no idea if it's true, or worse, he knows it's not? Is it a power play, a way for him to assert dominance over me?

Later in the morning, I ask for a show of hands in my class. Those who sleep in complete darkness don't even form an overwhelming majority. So my husband can't hide behind a numerical superiority. How could he have persuaded me that sleeping with the shutters closed simply went without saying?

My husband calls to tell me he forgot something he needs at work this afternoon. He was sure he had left it in his bag. It's a folder containing an important contract. I offer to bring it to him (near his office), which will give us an opportunity to eat lunch together. I'm still angry about the clementine, but I am mature enough to set my anger aside when necessary.

Back at home, I spend a long time putting together an outfit for the occasion, hesitating in front of the closet. I have an enormous amount of clothing. I don't buy a lot, but I keep everything. I am incapable of culling, donating, or throwing away: each piece of fabric is the relic of a bygone era, each article of clothing the memory of a former me, each closet shelf a time machine. I bought this

floral minidress the summer when I was twenty; Adrien
ripped it off of me before we made love all day long in
his dorm room, and I left with my cheeks red and my
hair tangled. This pair of jeans brings me back to when I
was running around in sneakers, impatient to catch the
47 bus because I was late for a meeting with my research
director to talk about my thesis. I bought this bag when
I started going out with the man who would become my
husband—it was the first luxury handbag I bought for
myself, an investment for the future, with money from
my first two teaching paychecks. Whether we were going
to a movie theater to see an art house film or on our way
to eat lunch at his parents' house on Sunday, this bag
gave me new confidence. And then there's the maternity
dress with the cherry print. I picture myself pregnant
and ready to burst, walking slowly and distractedly under the sun, all my time to myself and a chocolate eclair
in my hand (my obsession with eclairs was so intense
during my first pregnancy that I haven't been able to eat
them again since).

I change my blouse, swap my jeans for a skirt. In the
end I opt for a dress. I reapply my perfume, hoping that it
will finally unleash its danger, but it smells only of flowers
and cleanliness. I continue to perfume myself, spray after
spray, once, twice, ten times. But no poison, no passion
emerges from the overpriced flask. I can hardly breathe;
the sticky, heady rose scent is all over my body. I should

shower. I smash the flask against the floor with all my strength.

Gathering the pieces of glass, I cut my foot. A drop of blood falls onto the white rug, which I don't try to clean. The red stain pleases me. Finally, a bit of life in this immaculate interior. Before leaving, I blot my silk blouse with ink so I can have an excuse in case my husband asks me why I changed from this morning. I leave the stained blouse out on the bed to perfect my alibi. I'm not sure I'll manage to salvage it, even if I bring it to the dry cleaner tomorrow. It's too bad; that blouse looked good on me.

I'm about to apply another layer of mascara when I receive a text from my husband. I know it's him by the personal-ized ringtone. Of course, I chose something discreet—it's not like "La Vie en rose" plays every time my husband messages or calls. I'm not stupid. I chose a ringtone that's available on nearly every phone, two very simple notes (a D and a B). No one thinks anything of it, but I know immediately that those are the notes associated with a single contact in my phone: my husband. This trick helps me to avoid a lot of disappointment—hoping it's him, only to find that it's just a friend or family member.

Is my husband canceling our lunch? Does he no longer need the folder? Did I get dressed and made-up for nothing?

Is he telling me that he's not coming home tonight, that he's not coming home at all, that he's leaving me?

The beginning of the message is displayed on the screen. I can hardly believe my eyes. It begins: "Did you see the latest . . ." My husband is writing to comment on the latest actions of a politician that I heard something about on the radio earlier. I can't believe it. My husband texts me very rarely. He prefers a quick phone call, like he did earlier, to let me know he's going to get bread or ask me if I can drop off our son at his clarinet lesson. He calls me often, but texts are rare. And today, he's texting to talk politics when we're going to see each other in an hour. It makes no sense.

I would have *understood* if he were writing me to push back our lunch by a half hour. I would have *preferred* that he be writing to say he loves me and can't wait to see me. Or to offer an explanation for why he called me a clementine. But whatever my husband has to say about this politician—I really couldn't care less.

When we'd been going out for a few months, my husband left for a trip to Asia. France's elections were in full swing. I remember one night when he managed to call me from the hotel phone. We didn't have much time, and even so, he decided to bring up the election results.

He spoke passionately about the campaign that was nearing its end, the contents of the debates, the person he hoped would become president. I hadn't heard from him in several days; we'd had a hard time connecting by phone and the lack of news had been excruciating. What did I care whether the left won on Sunday? I hadn't even voted in the primary.

I make up a response to feign enthusiasm. I ponder how to conclude my message. I want to write to him: "See you soon, my love, can't wait." In the end, I settle for: "See you soon." Subdued and detached. Exactly how I want him to perceive me.

When I arrive, my husband isn't there. I'm early, it's not 1:00 yet. But my first thought is that he's not coming. He's left me for good now that he's realized I'm a cold mother and an overly demanding wife. He packed his things in two large suitcases, took the car, and rented an apartment downtown whose address he'll refuse to give me.

I try to reassure myself by repeating that it's not 1:00 yet. The only thing that eases my anxiety is knowing that my husband is punctual: I will know where I stand very soon.

I remember the day when we had to sign our home-owner's paperwork, just under ten years ago. We had an appointment with the notary on a Monday at 2:30, during our lunch break. I arrived fifteen minutes early. I waited for my husband in front of the entryway, nervously consulting my watch and phone. I tried to call him once at 2:25, a second time at 2:30. He didn't pick up. My husband was never late: clearly he had stood me up. He was getting cold feet, he wasn't ready, he had no desire for this life. I decided to ring the intercom at 2:35, tears in my eyes, shaking, prepared to tell our notary that he had to cancel everything. The notary welcomed me with a smile and brought me to his office, where my husband was waiting. He had already begun to initial the copies of the documents while he waited for me.

I think of that moment often. I picture my husband leaning over the stack of papers with a pen in his hand. So to calm myself down as I wait, I recall that scene, repeating to myself: "He was there all along."

People think it's all that anxious waiting that creates dependence and fuels passion. We imagine the object of desire as a man married to someone else, a man who doesn't answer the phone after a certain hour, who's inaccessible on Christmas or during the weeks of summer vacation. Passion is supposed to be born from passively waiting in front of the phone, the jealousy of knowing he's in bed with his wife, not knowing when you'll see each other next.

But to the adulterous lovers, to those who love each other from a distance, and to those who are no longer loved, I would like to say that love has never been a question of uncertainty or waiting, that regularity and reciprocity do not alter intensity. I would like to tell them that passion can also grow from domestic stability, from consistently punctual returns home, from the proof of commitment, from the repetition of daily life. I would like to tell them that the heart can also beat at set times.

It is exactly 1:00. I notice my husband's silhouette approaching in the distance. I'm not wearing my glasses (he prefers me without them), but I'm certain that it's him, even from where I am (he must be twenty meters away, maybe twenty-five). Is this the certain proof of love, to be able to distinguish with a glance your beloved's silhouette from all other silhouettes, even when you're nearsighted? Is visual hyperacuity a side effect of being in love? From what distance does love begin? When we recognize our beloved from ten, fifty, or a hundred meters away?

My husband suggested that we eat in an Italian restaurant a fifteen-minute walk from his office. Why go so far? Is he worried a colleague will see the two of us? Is he afraid that someone will ask him about his wife in front of me, bringing his infidelity to light? Is he ashamed of meeting me for a date? It's true that it's not very manly: a business lunch to discuss an important contract with Denmark would better match the image my husband aims to project. We sit on the terrace. I'm reassured: if he didn't want anyone to see us together, he would have chosen a table inside.

We've hardly sat down when my husband grabs the folder and slides it into his bag.

"It's why you came, after all!" he adds.

I don't argue, but it's not true. I'm happy to have come regardless. It's a shame that my husband has to forget an important contract for us to eat lunch together.

When the waitress brings us the menu, her youth and beauty rattle me. I don't let it show, and I rationalize: this young woman is very beautiful, but my husband would never leave me for a waitress. There's an English expression for this: wife material. When I met my husband, I knew right away that he would be excellent husband material. He had it all—the right social class, the right degree, a career, elegance. All the qualities of a husband for me and of a father for our future children. Frankly, this voluptuous waitress is not wife material. I don't doubt that she would make for a very good mistress. He could meet her at a hotel sometimes, relish her smooth skin, come between her breasts, but he would never introduce her to his parents. He would never bring her to a dinner with his colleagues, and he would never have a child with her. Basically, this waitress does not pose a serious threat.

When she comes back to take our order, I haven't had

time yet to look at the menu. My husband knows exactly what he wants: lasagna. Why doesn't he order meat like he usually does? In fifteen years, this is the first time he's ordered lasagna. He also has a question about the dessert and the wine. We just sat down—when did he have the time to think about all this? Did he look at the menu earlier, in preparation for our lunch (something I often do when I'm meeting him)? I feel rushed, so I order the same thing.

I don't know what we talk about, but the words flow naturally. Conversation between us has always been fluid. I remember the words that used to pour from his mouth during our first dates. Sometimes we even forgot to make love because we had so much to talk about. Maybe that's why we've always kissed less than other couples. Lovers who kiss all the time often do it to hide their lack of things to talk about: when one's mouth is glued to another's, it's difficult to have a deep discussion on the meaning of life. My husband and I have never felt a need to kiss to fill the void. In any case, that's what I tell myself when Nicolas and Louise kiss in the kitchen during our dinner: they finally have a few moments to speak in private, and instead they prefer to kiss. What a funny idea.

Our discussions are dense. Even with the years, they remain rich (in vocabulary, references, nuances, metaphors), which is vital. The fear of a lull has always terrorized me.

As a teenager, the relationship between Jean-Paul Sartre and Simone de Beauvoir was my model (except for their non-monogamy—open relationships are not my style). I would picture them in cafés, talking for hours and chain-smoking. I would fantasize about a marriage cemented by verbal and intellectual ping-pong, a union in which words played a leading role. With my husband, I always strive to finish his sentences and find new topics of conversation. I'm haunted by the idea that he might start to find me boring.

My husband is talking to me. I'm only half-listening, but he's talking to me, and that's enough. Hundreds of words, comments, exclamation points thrown into the air. I rehearse my next lines in advance to avoid silence between us at any cost. Our meals arrive just in time: I was struggling to think of what to bring up next.

I notice my husband's friendly tone with the waitress when she brings our lunch. What could account for such familiarity? Are they already sleeping together? Is that why he brought me to this restaurant? Does it excite my husband to introduce his wife to his mistress? What a perverse setup.

I still don't let anything show on my face. At first because I don't want to hint at my jealousy (revealing one's vulnerability is always an error). But also because, from a pragmatic point of view, there is a more important topic that I finally feel able to broach with him—the clementine. I have to pick my battles. I wait for the right moment in the conversation, then I begin:

"I've been thinking about what you said last night, about the clementine. I found it a bit harsh! I for one think I'm more of a blackberry, or a cherry."

"You're still hung up on that?" he responds, laughing.

He's laughing it off to shut down the conversation. My husband pauses and takes another sip of wine (is this his new way of changing the subject?). I've lost this battle.

We've just finished our meal when a man approaches our table. I recognize him as one of my husband's co-workers. He greets me, asks me how the children are doing. Couldn't he have asked my husband that on Monday morning by the coffee machine? Of the two of us, why is it always me who's asked about our homelife and vacation plans?

I am disturbed by this man who's with my husband every day at work. He knows my husband as a supervisor, mentor, and collaborator. It's an aspect of his personality that I never have access to myself. Is my husband appreciated, admired, or feared? I wonder what he's like in a professional context, what energy he gives off outside the house, with no wife or children around. I wonder what he's like when I'm not there to see him.

My husband invites him to join us for dessert (I pray that he doesn't spoil our date; he must hear my prayers, because he declines politely). Before leaving, he calls my husband by the name Arlequin. He understands by my startled gaze that I'm not in on the joke and explains that my husband's team gave him that nickname when they found out he was the one eating all the little colorful candies left out in their common kitchen. Of all the sweets, fruit, and drinks that the company provides for its employees, my husband always chooses those candies. This anecdote, seemingly benign, throws me for a loop. I was not aware of his sweet tooth. My husband has always preferred savory food.

When the check comes, my husband pays the bill. It's a minor detail perhaps, but this small act of care transforms our lunch into a gallant rendezvous. Then I notice that he leaves a frankly excessive tip. The slightly too-familiar tone with the waitress, the lasagna, the large tip: Has my husband fallen in love with another woman? Since it can't be the waitress, who is certainly not wife material, who is this other rival that I have to fear? Is it the euphoria of budding love that's making him spend carelessly and change his habits? There are, of course, other possible explanations for the shifts I've noticed in his behavior: maybe he's just happy to be eating lunch with me (the best-case scenario), relieved to have his file (probably true), or pleased by the mild weather this afternoon (it is nice out). But something has changed.

I can usually predict the meal my husband will order (everything but lasagna), the tip he'll leave on the table, and the way he'll thank the waitress on the way out. I know by heart the way he speaks. I know his tone, his intonations, his syntax. I can anticipate his words. I've even anticipated his sneezes. I know that he doesn't often eat sweet things. So how is it that he has so abruptly become a stranger to me?

On the way home, I cry. I cry about the clementine. I cry about the lasagna. I cry about all the ways my husband has hurt me. I cry and the passersby stare at me; you don't often see such a beautiful woman crying. I cry, and the worst part is that I'm sure the tears suit me. I'm sure I look like a Racinian heroine.

I think often of Phaedra, my favorite lover in literature (and there are plenty—the competition is fierce). I reread that particular Racine play often. The plot revolves around a single narrative axis. Phaedra is madly in love with Hippolytus. But not only is Hippolytus her son-in-law, he loves another woman, Aricia. He resists Phaedra's love, his heart doubly unattainable. Therefore the situation in which Phaedra finds herself is simple, and her sadness easy to understand. It is the universally recognizable sadness of impossible love.

The circumstances are sad, but I have never found

them tragic. Phaedra knows the reason for her sadness: her love is forbidden and incestuous as well as unrequited. Hippolytus is her son-in-law and he loves another woman. Phaedra must resign herself, die, forget, or live with it. She understands her situation; it's a clear predicament, easy to understand, and she can confide in her nurse, Oenone, and lament her pain in peace.

If I could speak to Phaedra, I would tell her that it is even more painful to love someone you already have. Unlike her, I have no real reason to cry. If I had to explain to a passerby why I'm crying, what could I possibly tell them? That I'm devastated because my husband thinks I'm a clementine? That I'm falling to pieces because he ordered lasagna? That I'm in tears because he left a substantial tip? Deep down, I know my tears have no reason to exist. Phaedra's tears are limpid as crystal; mine are monstrous.

Despite our differences, Phaedra and I have at least one thing in common: our rejection of love. Both of us would have preferred not to love. We suffer the consequences of an overly intense and inappropriate love. We feel no complacency about being a woman in love. No satisfaction with ourselves for experiencing such passion. I can't make allowances for my behavior when I work myself up into such a state.

I love. But don't think at the moment of loving you
I find myself innocent in my own eyes, or approve.

I have only one very close friend, Lucie. Our daughters have been inseparable since they started school, which has brought us closer. My husband has always been enough for me, and I don't need a best friend, but it just happened. At first, I was even opposed to the idea. I've always found it incredibly hard to make friends with other women. But since my husband got along well with Lucie's husband, the four of us started to hang out. For a year now, Lucie and I have even been meeting up every Saturday to play tennis together.

Although Lucie has become a friend, she is not a confidante. (I may be Phaedra, but she is not Oenone.) The fact that she knows my husband makes any truthful discussion of him impossible. Since we all started hanging out, she's often said to me that I found *the perfect man*, that I married *Prince Charming*.

When Lucie tells me about her problems with her husband, Pierre, she punctuates her confidences with assumptions that make me uneasy: "But you can't possibly understand, you don't have this kind of problem with your husband," or else: "Your husband would never do such a thing." She seems to know: my husband is different from hers. And even: my husband is different than all other husbands. She is so sure of herself that I've never tried to contradict her or ask her what she means by it.

Since I met my husband, my parents, sisters, and co-workers have always commented on my good fortune. "You're lucky," they tell me confidently. As if I won my husband in the lottery. As if I thwarted the statistics by marrying him. In other words, they are suggesting that he could have done better than me.

It's true. My husband's profession is more prestigious than mine, his degrees are more impressive than mine, he grew up in a bourgeois family, he plays tennis better than me, and he is handsome. I, on the other hand, come from a modest upbringing, I grew up in a working-class neighborhood, and I'm a high school English teacher. I speak and translate a language that nearly everyone understands (it's not Russian or Farsi—English isn't fascinating to anyone). Nothing about me really stands out.

Fortunately, I'm very beautiful. But my beauty won't last forever.

My husband could certainly have married better. Even so, I am embarrassed that this imbalance is so obvious to everyone else. I am mostly embarrassed that they speak about it so freely, that it's socially acceptable to announce to me with no shame that I'm "lucky." To my knowledge, no one has ever told my husband that he's "lucky" to have me.

It's this inequality between me and my husband that stops me from confiding in Lucie. She would surely tell me that I'm worrying over nothing, that my husband is faithful and that he loves me, that he's a wonderful partner and father. She would remind me that *I have it all* (another expression that my loved ones tend to use to describe my life). Basically, she would tell me that she doesn't see the problem.

I've spoken to someone about my situation only once. It was four years ago, on a trip to the mountains. I had hit it off with an Italian woman who was staying in the same hotel as us. It was her first trip to the resort and I knew that I would probably never see her again. That morning, we agreed to meet at the hotel pool. Seated on the edge, legs in the water up to our knees, we stared straight ahead as though we were watching our children swim, even though we were the only ones by the empty pool. Opposite us, on the other side of the large bay windows, the first skiers descended the trails, tracing pretty curves on the snowy mountains. I confided in her without ever meeting her gaze. She didn't say a word and let me finish. She wasn't looking at me, her feet swaying in the water. I prayed that she wouldn't answer me in stock phrases. Especially not consoling words or false compassion. I wanted her to tell me what to do so badly.

After a few minutes, she said the following words, which I've never forgotten:

"I think you're way off the mark. You've never thought that maybe your husband loves you more than you love him? You say that you're madly in love with him, but don't you think he's actually the one who's really in love? Between the two of you, he's the one whose love has moved beyond the passionate honeymoon phase. You're still living in the obsessive stage that normally only lasts the first few months of a relationship. You don't even trust him, as though you've built nothing together. Maybe things aren't exactly how you'd like them to be, but you said it yourself: your husband supports you, knows you, respects you, and loves you. I think you've got it all wrong. Your husband is the infatuated one. Not you. You don't even really love him."

Her words floated over the empty pool. I didn't respond. I got up and dove in. How could she claim I didn't love my husband when my problem was precisely that I loved him too much? I promised myself never to confide in anyone again.

However, something in her words rang true. Maybe that's what hurt me so much. There was a strange resonance with the second part of my favorite Marguerite Duras quote: "never loved, though I thought I loved." It's even possible that she spoke these words, in this order: "you never loved your husband, though you thought you loved him." Had she also read *The Lover*? I didn't dare ask.

We didn't speak again for the rest of the trip. But during our last night at the resort, I thought I saw her whisper something in my husband's ear.

The car door closes, the mailbox opens, the key turns in the lock: it's 7:30 p.m. My heart is racing, I come alive. Life resumes.

Just before he enters, I go to the second-floor window and watch him cross the flowery driveway to determine whether he seems happy or not to be home. He doesn't seem in any kind of hurry, nor does he fix his hair before opening the door, but he has a slight smile on his lips. My husband is always sending me contradictory signals.

I go back downstairs to welcome him. The smell of the chicken roasting perfects this scene, which I've already played out several times in my head. My husband kisses the children on the forehead and me on the cheek. His false modesty revolts me. They're not stupid, they know their parents kiss on the mouth, so why does he refuse to do it in front of them? It worries me that my husband isn't more effusive: What do my children think of our relationship? Do they believe that their father is in love with me? They're only children, but they are nevertheless the most privileged witnesses of our love. And they say that children can sense this kind of thing, that they're emotional sponges—something to do with mirror neurons. I'd like to ask them, but I haven't found a way to broach the subject. Maybe we'll be able to discuss it more easily when they're teenagers. Will we finally be able to talk about love and the meaning of life at the dinner table?

Among all the rituals of shared life, the very regulated choreography of the family meal is the one that annoys me the most. This afternoon, we were two lovers sitting on a restaurant terrace; passersby could have taken us for two coworkers burning with desire for each other who have not yet dared make the first move, or two former lovers trying to say goodbye for good (impossible to know for certain from the outside). Tonight, however, the roles we perform are unambiguous: we are two parents having dinner with their children, a classic family portrayal. I play the mother and he the father. And I miss my husband.

Everyone knows their part. My husband keeps the dinner lively, conducting the conversation, as though it's his mission to make our children speak. At least I don't have to dread a lull. He asks them questions, then asks again, demanding precision, requesting that they rephrase what they've said, surveying the coherent artic- ulation of their thoughts: school, extracurriculars, their education, their music classes, the end-of-year concert at the conservatory. As for me, I smile at them with as much benevolence as I'm capable of as I listen to them speak. Because, to be honest, what's shared over dinner is of very little interest to me. I ask my husband about his day, but his responses are vague. I can't even be angry at him about it. He can't give me the details of the complicated case he's working on, share his concern over his parents' health, or speak openly about his desires: not in front of the children. At their age, they're old enough to under- stand but too young to care. We speak without anything important ever being said around our table, which pro- foundly frustrates and bores me.

Fortunately, my children have always gone to bed earlier than other kids their age. I've reminded them hundreds of times of the importance of a good night's sleep. I've described in great detail all the essential pro- cesses that occur overnight: their muscles relax and rest, their brain integrates and sorts the memories of the day, their imagination works overtime to churn out vibrant dreams, their growth hormones spread through their bodies to make them taller. And so my children like to go to bed early.

In reality, encouraging my children's sleep is an egotistical mission, calculated for my own purposes, so that
I can spend several hours alone with my husband each
night. But the older my children get, the later their bed-
time is pushed back and, inevitably, the time spent alone
with my husband diminishes. Miserable and powerless,
I witness the transformation of our couple into a family.

My children are old enough now to read alone in their
beds, but my husband continues to read a few pages with
them every night. When they were young, he would tell
them stories about the kings of France. He would begin
with the Merovingian dynasty, then the Carolingian, then
the Direct Capetians and the Valois. Finally, he would
arrive at the Bourbons and begin again. He followed the
chapters of a large red book with pages worn from being
turned so many times, but the book was only a pretext,
the starting point for a story that he embellished with
new anecdotes each time (Louis XIII's stutter, the gossip of
Louis XIV's court, the swift ascension of Nicolas Fouquet)
and various questions (Who was the last son of Louis IX?
Diane de Poitiers was whose favorite? What queen was responsible for the Palais du Luxembourg?). These detours
into dates, characters, and battles enraptured our children.
My husband never told them the same story twice.

I didn't like when the story revolved around Henri IV,

who was notoriously unfaithful. I preferred the adventures of Louis XV. He was a mediocre king, true, but at least he remained faithful to the same mistress all his life. But my favorite story takes place on the other bank of the Rhine: the story of General Bismarck, who loved his wife with a constancy and fervor unequaled in history. Never a dalliance, even when his military campaigns distanced him from his beloved for months on end.

When we were a young couple with no children, my husband would read me love poems by Paul Éluard and passages from *In Search of Lost Time* on Sunday morning while we drank our coffee in bed. Now he reads aloud to our children. Twentieth-century poetry and Marcel Proust have left the bedroom and obediently resumed their place in the living room library.

I also read many stories to our children when they were little. But it came less naturally for me than for my husband. I never struck the right tone and I could never imitate the voices of the characters as well as him. The very act made me uncomfortable: it was impossible for me to gauge what their young minds understood of the adventures I was recounting to them, whether I was going too fast or too slow. At night in their bedroom, time stretched on and the books seemed endless.

Now my daughter is seven, almost eight. When I read her a story, I try to choose one in which there's no prince, no romance. I buy her books with independent heroines who defy dragons, sail warships, dig up dinosaur bones. Choosing such a story is part of the painful responsibility I feel toward my daughter. I want to prevent her at all costs from making the same mistakes as I did.

I love our children, that goes without saying. I love them, but still, I would rather have not had them. I love them, but I would rather have lived alone with my husband. Today, I think I can say with certainty that I could survive the death of one of my children, but not of my husband.

Giving him a child brought us closer. Especially at the beginning, when the three of us were living in isolation. It was a commitment for life (I would always be the mother of his children) and a precious complicity (the two of us shared the difficult nights when our son's ear infection kept us awake till dawn). This little boy was one more thing we had in common, an inexhaustible topic of conversation, the proof and the concretization of his love for me. But it wasn't enough to inspire as much love for my son as it should have.

When my husband went back to work and I found myself home alone with a newborn, I felt like a prisoner, trapped in the role of mother, which I had no desire to play and for which I had no talent. I felt nothing when this infant was sleeping against my shoulder. Later on, I never knew what to say to our children on the way back from school. No maternal instinct for me. I never managed to appear fascinated like the other parents did when their children recounted their days. I never managed to be interested in their games, their problems, their friendships. I never managed to slow myself down to their pace; although now my children move at a reasonable speed, for a long time their slowness exasperated me. My daughter in the stroller, my son walking next to us, me always repeating, "Don't let go of the stroller, always keep your hand on it!" Going between daycare and the house (724 meters) felt like going from Paris to Tokyo (9,710 kilometers).

I love my children, but their presence weighs on me. Not being able to speak about anything of substance at night around the table. Having to wait for them to be asleep to make love with my husband. Counting on one hand the weekends I've spent alone with him in the last ten years. Losing time when we go places: when we're together, I walk 4.7 kilometers per hour, while alone I walk 6.8. Not to mention my body, which I watched deform during my pregnancies (fortunately, it was a temporary distortion, as I was able to lose all the weight I'd gained). Obviously I chose not to breastfeed my children: I was too attached to the perkiness of my chest to give up such an important aspect of my femininity for them.

As a mother, I'm not present enough, devoted enough, attentive enough. When I go to pick up my children at school, there is always a group of parents talking in a corner. I wave to them and act as though I'm in a hurry, which allows me to avoid saying hello. In reality, I'm afraid that they'll ask me to work a booth at the school party, or that they'll realize over the course of a conversation that I don't know the names of their children, even though they always ask me about mine.

I read somewhere that there are three kinds of women: the woman in love, the mistress, and the mother. That seems right to me. I spent my childhood and adolescence being the woman in love: my dreams for the future were inspired by sappy novels, and the only films I deemed worthy of my interest were those that portrayed love stories. The endings didn't matter to me, as long as the love was passionate. As a young woman, I continued my search for a great love. I still had no desire to be a mistress—loving without any commitment held no appeal. And then when I had children, I never moved to the next stage. I never changed categories to become a mother.

I do my best, but most of the time I'm too busy being in love to be a good mother.

My husband lowers the volume of the music so as not to wake the children. The chorus repeats as though to taunt me with the idea that loving is easy. My husband listens to this Rex Orange County song on repeat. Does he do it on purpose to emphasize my inability to love like everyone else? Perhaps instead he's trying to show me the way, send me a subtle message—look, loving can be easy, if you let it be—but I doubt it. I have a tendency to see the negative in everything, but his song choices are rarely kind. And English-language pop is often the start of our iciest nights.

My husband is always the one who chooses the music. He makes the playlist for our love life and regularly updates the soundtrack of our family life. With a click, he sets the tone, deciding whether the ambience will be melancholic or festive, militant or romantic. Over time,

I've even learned to detect whether he's in a good or bad mood based on the song. I choose the music only when I'm in my car; when I'm alone, I listen to whatever songs are on the radio, and I still buy CDs for my drives. (Right now, I'm listening to a freckled musician who sings wonderfully about his divorce. Weirdly enough, the album is called *Paradise*.)

While my husband takes his shower, I wait on the sofa. I feel like a piece of the furniture. With the music as background noise and the decorating magazines left on the coffee table to help pass the time, it's like I'm in a waiting room. I flip through *The Lover* with the tips of my fingers without reading it.

When my husband finally joins me again, I close the book. Systematically, when my husband enters the room, I put down my book, turn off the radio, set aside my work, switch off the television. Out of reflex, I stop what I'm doing. I make myself available.

My husband puts on a jazz standard. But it's not just any song. This was our first dance song on our wedding night. How could I possibly think his song choices are random when the proof is undeniable?

My husband didn't help pick out the color of the wedding announcements, nor did he have any real opinions on the menu. However, he had insisted on picking out the song for our first dance, saying, "I want 'Day by Day.'" I had suggested an acoustic version of "Sweep Me Off My Feet" instead—the song from the night we first met, I liked the symbolism of it—but he refused. He repeated a hundred times that "Day by Day" was the most beautiful love song ever written. I listened to it a hundred times without ever being able to grasp its beauty.

The idea is simplistic: Frank Sinatra sings that he is falling more in love each day.

How could my husband subscribe to such a dangerous idea? I've always loved my husband unconditionally. Since day one, with the same intensity, and nothing has ever changed it. I thought, mistakenly, that this was also how my husband thought of marriage—before I heard the words of that song. The terrible truth was laid bare: his love for me was still growing two years after we met, and he found this variation of sentiment normal. If my husband thought he would always love me more as time went on, didn't that mean that he would never really love me in the present? On the dance floor, in front of our friends and family, this quotation by the philosopher Blaise Pascal came back to me with terror: "If we are always preparing to be happy, it is inevitable that we will never be so."

I often look through the pages of our wedding photo

album, on the top shelf of our library; am I the only one who sees the two tears of sadness in the corners of my eyes while I'm in his arms during our first dance?

My husband shuts off the music and turns on the television. I would prefer that we talk, but I stay silent. Less than an hour earlier, he had said good night to our children and told them a final story in a way only he knows how to do. He used the right tone, he laughed, he was affectionate. But now that we're finally alone, he seems completely emptied out. There is nothing left of him; he's as hollow as a plastic water bottle. Daily life exhausts him. If he can't spend the remainder of the night alone, relaxing without having to answer to anyone, then my husband at least needs peace and quiet. On weeknights, I can't speak too loudly, can't broach serious topics of conversation, can't stimulate him. The only thing to do is to let him rest.

He's used to my presence. He's not surprised to see me sitting next to him on the sofa. When we're in the same room, he isn't thinking about the strength of our love or the improbable alignment of circumstances that led to us meeting. He doesn't jump when I move. He doesn't wonder whether I'm leaving for good when I go to the kitchen to make a cup of tea. His body doesn't lean toward mine to make sure it's real.

I feign interest in the movie, but all my attention is concentrated on a single mission: placing my hand on his. I slide my fingers beneath his palm. But two minutes later, my husband changes position and lets go of my hand.

Ah! do not run away yet!
Leave it, let my hand be forgotten in your hand!

Romeo's beseeching of Juliet seems right to me. The Gounod opera is reenacted on my sofa several nights per week.

I wish I had the courage to turn to him and shout that our meeting was a miracle. Make him understand that my hand in his is the most beautiful sight he'll ever witness. How could I become familiar to him so quickly? After the first months of enchantment, I observed, powerless, the merging of our lives, which only wound up distancing us even more. The emotionally loaded looks and the awkward gestures were replaced by a gentle complicity. Passion was snuffed out to make room for the quotidian.

In the beginning, our romantic landscape was like an infinite stretch of dunes; it evoked the danger of barrenness, the immensity of the starry sky, the stifling heat of the day, and the sudden cold of the night. Then the desert became a lake: a flat, smooth expanse. I saw my husband become so used to my presence that he no longer found it miraculous.

As I'm counting how long my husband keeps his arm on my knee (I'm satisfied when it lasts more than two minutes), he suddenly takes out his phone from his pocket. Is he bored? I don't understand his need to be in contact with the outside world when I'm right next to him. How could he tap away on his keyboard in my presence? What could be more important right now?

I think of all the slights I've endured since Monday, which continue tonight. I was right—pop music in English is never a good sign. As evidenced by the fact that he has his phone out when I'm right next to him. As evidenced by the fact that he didn't put his hand back on mine and our bodies are no longer touching, not even our knees. As evidenced by the fact that he doesn't ask me how my translation is going. As evidenced by the fact that he doesn't thank me again for bringing his folder this afternoon. As evidenced by the fact that he still hasn't apologized for turning me into a clementine. As evidenced by the fact that he doesn't offer to make an exception and leave the shutters open tonight. As evidenced by the fact that he doesn't tell me that our children are wonderful and that our life together is a blessing.

I begin to fantasize about my husband turning toward me suddenly and touching my legs. We'd exchange a few affectionate words as he moved his hand along my thigh. He'd turn me over on the sofa, pull off my dress, violently press his hand against my mouth, and shove his cock between my wet thighs. I imagine it so vividly, but my husband doesn't make any move at all, because he's too busy watching TV.

He changes the channel, then turns the TV off entirely. This unilateral control over the remote leaves me wondering: Is my husband authoritarian? He doesn't ask me whether I want to watch the movie. He doesn't say, as other husbands surely do, "Should we turn it off?" He never says the transitional phrases that signal the conclusion of one activity and the beginning of another, like "Should we go to bed?" He acts without giving any advance notice: he grabs the remote, turns off the television, stands up, and goes to bed. He doesn't put words to things. I'm left to piece it together on my own.

I'm convinced that if I were to put a camera in Nicolas and Louise's living room, or in Lucie and Pierre's, I would witness a completely different scene. At a certain point in the evening, one of them would ask the other if they can turn off the TV, or say that they're tired and want to go to bed. Perhaps I would even see their bodies draw closer once the television is off. Watch them kiss and touch.

That's when my husband says to me, word for word:

"I don't know what's going on these days. It's still March weather even though it's already the beginning of June. It's like there aren't any seasons anymore!"

I stand up so that he doesn't notice my tears and go to boil some water to make myself another tea. The sound will cover up that of my tears (even if this kind of crying is generally silent). When my husband talks to me about the rain or sun, when he doesn't take my hand, when he turns me into a clementine, when he keeps his eyes open during a kiss, I am as vulnerable as a sixteen-year-old— as a six-year-old, even.

I don't know what's going on these days. It's still March weather even though it's already the beginning of June. It's like there aren't any seasons anymore! It is unacceptable that my husband would talk to me about the weather. It is unacceptable that we have nothing else to say to each other. Not after all my efforts to maintain stimulating and wide-ranging conversations between us.

I don't know what's going on these days. It's still March weather even though it's already the beginning of June. It's like there aren't any seasons anymore! Today I have the proof. We were a rocket headed for space, our love escaping the Earth's magnetic field. Now we're more like a freight train—slow, heavy, monotonous.

Drying my tears, I try to muster up the courage to join him in the bedroom. I often wonder whether my husband purposely heads to bed first so as not to have to turn off all the lights behind him. For the ambience tonight, I used what I could find (three candles and a small lamp), since the floor lamp broke this afternoon; at least it won't ruin any more nights with my husband with its overly aggressive light.

I take advantage of being alone to write a few lines in my notebook. Of course I record how he withdrew his hand from mine just now on the sofa, how he took his phone from his pocket when I was right next to him. Once more, writing calms me down.

Before going upstairs, I use the bathroom on the ground floor. A real blessing. Upstairs, the bathroom is right next to our bedroom, which means I have to go downstairs under the guise of making myself a cup of tea or looking for the book I'm reading, or else I say that I forgot to run the dishwasher. Because after fifteen years of life together, I still prefer to lie, to make myself sick, to wait to go at school or at a restaurant—whatever I have to do so that my husband never hears me go to the bathroom.

Once again I won't escape it. As I'm trying to fall asleep, my entire body starts to itch, like there's an insect moving around on my skin faster than my nails can scratch. Ever since I met my husband, I've had trouble sleeping. I'm never as anxious as when I try to sleep. And yet I thought marriage would be the most powerful sleeping aid: I pictured myself as a young, radiant, contented bride, asleep within a few minutes every night, full of a new serenity, my complexion glowing (similar in my imagination to a pregnant woman, but I was wrong about that, too). I pinned a great deal of hope on our legal union, thinking it would erase all my fears, in particular my nocturnal anguish. I thought that commitment would finally confirm my husband's love for me, authenticating it once and for all, as a jeweler might do upon examining a necklace: "Yes, madame, I'm sure of it: it's definitely gold."

In reality, marriage didn't calm me down. I realized at the very moment we said "I do" that my husband could still divorce me. Then I hoped that he would want to buy a house with me, and then have a child with me, certain that these acts would be more solid than a contract signed at city hall or a promise made before God. I was constantly awaiting the next step. I discovered a world of proofs of love, with commitment everywhere and love nowhere. And fifteen years after our first date, I still sleep just as poorly.

With the exception of my unexplained itching and my all-consuming passion for my husband, my life is perfectly normal. Nothing out of order. No psychological incoherence, no mania, no flagrant signs of a personality disorder. I eat a balanced diet, I'm not overly anxious about my children, I have no problem coming during sex, I'm not a hypochondriac. My friends like me, my coworkers appreciate me, I have no particular sexual fetishes, I'm not afraid of being home alone at night, I've forgiven my parents for their mistakes, I'm close to my sisters, I'm not envious, I'm not distracted, I have no problems with alcohol, and I smoke only very occasionally.

But I am madly in love with my husband and my entire body starts to itch in bed at night.

To calm myself down, I start off by whispering the name of my husband three or four times, like a short prayer. That's not enough, so I choose a question. It's a mental game I've been playing since childhood. The questions have evolved over time, but the idea remains the same: think of a question, and search for the answer until I'm exhausted.

As a little girl, I would ask myself: If I made a list of my five best friends, who would they be and in what order? If I could exchange my mother for another mother, whom would I choose?

As a teenager, I moved on to other scenarios: If I could buy anything I wanted for a day, what stores would I go to? If I could change three aspects of my physical appearance and replace them with the features of three other girls, who would I decide to swap my nose or butt with?

As a young woman, my questions continued to evolve: If I could live in my dream home, what would it look like? Then, every night, I would imagine a different room: the kitchen, the living room, the bathroom, the bedroom, until I had dreamed up the perfect house. I would also think a lot about the future *man of my dreams*. At night in my bed, I would draw his portrait: Would he be blond or brunet? What would his profession be? Actor or engineer? Doctor or musician?

Now there are several questions I use to fall asleep at night: If I could wake up tomorrow at age ten, knowing what I know today, what would I do differently? If I could possess a single magical power, what would it be?

One thing is for sure: if I could wake up tomorrow as a ten-year-old again, I would study to be an astrophysicist or an astronaut, learn Latin and Greek, become a fencing champion. And above all: no crushes in elementary school, no boyfriend as a teenager, no great love story before marriage. I wouldn't waste a minute being in love.

Tonight, I decide that if I could have one magical power, I would want to control dreams. I would inflict horrible nightmares on anyone who posed a threat to me, and meddle in my husband's sleep to make him dream of me each night. I would imbue the fear of losing me into his subconscious, constructing a world in which I leave him for another man and he dies of sadness. I would show him my body in its most magnificent form so that he would never stop desiring me, and our house looking its best so that he would always want to stay. I would weave beautiful images of us into each of his nights so that he would continue loving me.

But I don't have this power. So tonight, I speak to him while he's asleep. I lean close to his ear and whisper to him that he could never live without me. I know by the sound of his breathing that he's asleep; I recognize his unconscious face. But I also know that when he wakes up, my words will have taken hold. It's like when a newborn hears their parents arguing or being affectionate. The newborn is in their crib, unable to see past the tip of their nose, but the conversations in the distance become engraved somewhere in them.

My husband's breathing is now like the sound of the sea: the waves of his breath swell, retreat, return. His sighs mimic and outline the horizon as I continue to whisper his dreams, which are also mine, the night my only witness.

Thursday.

My husband woke me up last night by touching my shoulder. In the dark of the bedroom, I heard him say again and again that he loves me. He insisted: "I love you, I love you so much, I love you." It's everything I've ever dreamed of.

I didn't fall back asleep right away, and I noticed that my husband and I were breathing in and out with the same rhythm. When we're awake, we don't breathe at the same speed—I've already checked. We aren't the same size, so his lungs are larger than mine; they require more air. But our separate rhythms must have synchronized during the night: my breath accelerated, while his slowed to merge with mine. Is there a greater symbol of love than two breaths matching up in sleep?

I know that I'm not just making this up deliriously.

There are very serious articles on the topic: sharing a life with someone modifies our biological rhythm—the speed of our heartbeat, the tempo of our breathing, the rate of our digestion. It's also for these physiological reasons that my husband's absence can be so painful: my body is in withdrawal.

This morning, I am pleasantly surprised by the shower temperature: the water is unusually hot. I think back to last night. It was definitely my husband who showered last. Was he trying to do the same thing I did on Tuesday morning? Shower with the water the way I like it to immerse himself in my aquatic universe? That he might have had the same idea delights me. I forget just how thoughtful my husband can be when he feels like it.

Euphoric from his late-night declaration and the shower temperature, I leave the shutters closed and get dressed in the dark without batting an eye: my husband made a gesture toward me, so I am ready to make an effort in return. I choose a long yellow skirt, happy to match the color of my outfit to the day that's about to begin.

My yellow Thursday starts joyfully. I'm hungry. I prepare myself a large, sweet breakfast (I eat sweet things only when I'm in a good mood): two pieces of toast with a thick layer of butter and jam, which I dip into a mug of hot chocolate. I even peel two clementines, my joy slightly tempering my bitterness toward this fruit.

I don't react when my husband calls to me from the bedroom. I heard his question perfectly well, but I ignore it; it's hard, but it's what I have to do. Whenever I actually don't hear what he says to me, though, I can't help asking him to repeat himself. The idea that his words might evaporate in the air is unbearable to me. What if he were saying something important?

I remember his phone calls during his trip to Asia a few months after we met. The connection was so bad that I lost hundreds of his words with each call. Since I couldn't ask him to repeat himself more than a certain number of times without seeming silly, I had to settle for leaving those words behind us, forever abandoned to oblivion along the underwater phone lines somewhere between Egypt and the Indian coast.

Couples who don't love each other anymore don't care about not catching everything. They think of their exchanges as a text with many holes, and are unbothered by it; they say it's no big deal, they'll fill in the gaps later. I think the need to be exhaustive is proof of love: not wanting to lose a single word.

I check my hair a final time in front of the large

entryway mirror. On the table is some change, our keys intertwined in the ceramic bowl, a tube of lipstick, two baptism announcements—and my notebook of scientific vocabulary that I was looking for everywhere on Tuesday. How could I have missed it? Actually, I know exactly why I didn't see it before, and the reason makes me smile.

My smile lasts all the way to school. I teach with conviction, I move more spryly than usual between the desks, I speak louder. I'm more immersed, more involved, more patient, too; even my accent seems more fluid and my writing straighter on the whiteboard. In my classroom, the air seems more robust, the oxygen more nourishing.

During break, my husband tries to call me. I don't pick up on his first two tries (once again, it's hard, but that's the rule). I call him back five minutes later and we talk about my faculty meeting tonight at school. I remind him that he needs to bring the kids to the conservatory later.

My good mood is written all over my face. People tell me that I'm glowing, and I get compliments on my skirt. I eat with a coworker I like. We speak about our students (interesting), our husbands (my favorite part), our children (immediately less interesting).

My husband's nocturnal declaration of love explains my joy, but the large smile that's been on my face since this morning is also because it's Thursday. Thursday is like a second Monday. It's a new beginning, the end of intermission, the swimmer kicking the pool wall to flip and head back in the other direction, the picnic halfway through the hike.

Then, at 1:00, I'm invaded by doubt. A devastating, hyperbolic doubt. What actually happened last night? Did my husband really say those words? Or did I dream them? But I remember it so perfectly: "I love you, I love you so much, I love you." "I love you," then "I love you so much," then once again "I love you." I can still distinctly hear his voice. He didn't say it once, but three times. I couldn't be mistaken three times over. I couldn't have dreamed for so long.

Sweep me off my feet, please,
Sweep me off my feet now.

In class, we're working on a translation. The most stimulating exercise: try by any means possible to translate the untranslatable, when the exact equivalent doesn't exist in French and we have to cobble something together.

Sweep me off my feet. If we translate word for word,

we come up with *balaie-moi de mes pieds*, but that doesn't mean anything. It's more like *renverse-moi*, "bowl me over," but then we lose the idea of the feet and being anchored to the ground. Another possibility: *fais-moi perdre pied*, "make me lose my footing," but now we lose the idea of the gesture and the fall. Impossible to get everything in a single phrase. *Sweep me off my feet*: *bouscule-moi*, "knock me over." *Fais-moi perdre l'équilibre et tomber*, "make me lose my balance and fall down." *Décroche-moi du sol*, "detach me from the ground." *Déracine-moi*, "uproot me." *Fais basculer ce qui me faisait encore tenir debout*, "topple what is keeping me standing." *Pousse-moi, je veux dégringoler et assister à ma propre chute*, "push me, I want to plummet and witness my own fall." It's a demand, uttered in the imperative: *Sweep me off my feet, please.* Make me fall in love with you, please. *Sweep me off my feet now.* Make me fall in love with you, now.

This phrase describes the instant that precedes the encounter, just before the plummeting, when we summon love. Because you never meet the love of your life out of nowhere, as unexpected as it might seem. We must be, even unconsciously, prepared to meet someone. It's that state of impatience that my students and I debate.

I purposely choose texts about love or existential dilemmas, because the debates that arise with my students feed my inner life. Between fifteen and eighteen years old, emotions are heightened; it's the age when you first fall passionately in love. So my students know very well what it's all about—surely better than their parents. This way, I guarantee a certain number of profound conversations during my week. Everywhere else, I feel like I speak only about logistics and practicalities (vacation, interior decoration, meal choices, private or public school). Adult conversations typically revolve around domestic concerns more than metaphysical ones.

Sweep me off my feet, please,
Sweep me off my feet now.

I didn't choose these lyrics at random. My husband and I met while this song was playing. I had begrudgingly agreed to go with a friend to see an English band I'd never heard of. The music was super loud and we had a hard time hearing each other, but when a stranger leaned toward me to tell me his name, I immediately fell in love with him. His first name seemed to be a good omen: full of promise and reassuring at the same time. The first name of a lover, of a husband. What came next proved me right. The way we met was so wonderful that sometimes I feel like it's the real story, and our relationship merely an endless footnote.

As we spoke our first words (the idea that there was once a world in which my husband and I had only ever exchanged ten words makes me dizzy—how many are we at now?), the singer repeated over his guitar riffs those words that I've never forgotten: *Sweep me off my feet, please, Sweep me off my feet now.*

That night, my husband was with one of his friends. I think often about that man who was lucky enough to witness our first encounter. I so wish I could watch the scene from his point of view. Could he already anticipate the importance that night would come to have in our lives? Can you tell from the outside when something is a casual fling versus when something is destined to upend an entire existence? Was the air around us charged with electricity, ready to react to the slightest spark?

That man died in a car accident the following year, so I was never able to ask for his version of events. A part of the narrative of our origins, an essential aspect of our romantic cosmogony, was stolen from me. His death might explain certain issues I've have with my husband since: How can we know where we're going if we don't know where we're coming from? So to make up for it, every year I study those song lyrics with my students, and I continue to try to pierce the mystery that surrounds any first encounter.

I finish the translation of the exchange of vows my class began on Monday. The "I do" becomes *Je le veux*, which still produces the same effect, although I notice that the girls are more receptive to it than the boys.

"It's a beautiful declaration of love. The woman seems very in love with her husband," one of my students comments.

I'm glad I kept the vows I wrote thirteen years ago for my husband: it's a good translation exercise for my students, a chance to review the use of the auxiliary. I wasn't able to recite my vows on the day of our wedding, after months of writing and research. I had consulted some fifty articles, read dozens of books on the subject, watched countless romantic comedies, filled a thick notebook with all my research and drafts; it would have been a waste not to do anything with them. I transformed a romantic failure into a pedagogical success: Who says I don't know how to bounce back? The more an educator is personally invested in the contents of their course, the better their teaching.

My husband and I were married in a château in the middle of a vineyard. It was the wedding I had always dreamed of as a young girl: hundreds of guests, my blond hair in an elegant bun, a sumptuous dress that spun with each of my movements, tables illuminated in the night with lanterns of all colors. Of course I had some apprehension—my working-class parents sat at the same table as my husband's bourgeois parents—but in the end, if my in-laws didn't enjoy themselves, they hid it well.

Enamored with the Anglo-Saxon universe, I insisted that there be an exchange of vows, including a speech, handwritten by my husband, in which he would explain why he was so happy to be marrying me. I even imagined that we would frame our two texts and hang them in our bedroom after. I couldn't fathom the idea of my husband not publicly expressing his love. By nature an introvert, he never waxed poetic about his passion for me. So what was the good in having a wedding if it wasn't an opportunity to receive a declaration of love from my husband? I sensed even then that I would need it to comfort me during the nights of doubt to come.

I spent weeks pushing for it with my future husband, then with my in-laws. The four pillars of Catholic marriage and vows in front of the priest held little value for me. I agreed to perform those rituals, but they have nothing to do with love, passion, commitment. I wanted an exchange of vows like in American movies. My mother-in-law was surprised—it wasn't traditional—but she pretended to hear me out so as not to hurt my feelings. I explained that it was important for me. I even thought about inventing ancestors in the United States to justify my attachment to the custom. My in-laws finally suggested that we could exchange vows at the start of the meal, after the toasts.

The day of the wedding, everything seemed to be going smoothly: the dress, the weather, my skin. As planned, the guests gave their speeches before the dinner, blending humor and sincerity (a must for such an occasion). Then came the exchange of vows. My husband grabbed the microphone, thanked our loved ones for being there, said a word for those who couldn't be there with us that night. Then he turned to me:

"It was important for my wife that we take the time to share our joy at being together. To speak these words aloud, in front of our loved ones. So that's what I'll do: I love you, my wife. I will always love you. I am the happiest man to have met the most beautiful woman in the world."

Applause. Tears in our parents' eyes. In my hand, the vows I had spent months writing. My husband handed me the microphone, but I didn't unfold the paper crumpled between my fingers. He had only said a few words; it would have been ridiculous for me to read my speech (which was seven minutes long; I had practiced and timed it). So I thanked the guests for coming once more, and I told my husband much too solemnly that I was happy to be his wife and that I would always love him. I was frozen to the spot, unable to say anything about the beauty of our meeting two years prior, of our endless conversations on café terraces in the months that followed, of the night when we danced between boxes in the apartment we had just moved into.

"I am the happiest man to have met the most beautiful woman in the world": I would have appreciated not being reduced to my physical appearance and instead complimented on my personality or the sharpness of my intellect. Everyone knows that beauty doesn't last a lifetime, unlike the bonds of marriage.

"I love you, my wife. I will always love you": simplicity and reserve. Those two words suit him well, and thus so did his vows (if we can even call them vows). Simplicity and reserve are fine. But I had dreamed of gravitas and effusiveness. At that moment, I thought to myself that perhaps he was too young and immature to get married. If he couldn't express the profound reasons for his love for me, perhaps it was because he had not yet identified them? He found me beautiful and kind: Was that enough for him, and so he hadn't looked any further, hadn't asked himself the question? "I love you, my wife. I will always love you": a lovely line, but a bit flimsy for a lifelong pledge. I seriously wondered whether he had grasped the level of commitment he had just taken in marrying me.

I still have the same pang in my heart when I turn on my phone after an hour of class and see that my husband hasn't called. So I decide to call him myself. As it rings, I feel my blood pressure rise, my heart race, adrenaline pump through my amygdala. I desperately need to know: Darling, did you tell me you loved me last night? He picks up. We chat for a few minutes. Casually I tell him about my last class, then I take the plunge. I bring up his declaration. My husband doesn't know what I'm talking about. I explain. I flirt with humiliation and then finally say it outright: "Didn't you tell me you loved me last night?" The response is cutting and definitive: "No."

I so needed him to remember. I so needed it to be true. The problem is that I often hear my husband tell me he loves me. It happened last month, too. I asked him if he remembered the conversation we'd had in the bathroom that morning. Since he didn't know what I was referring to, I was forced to spell it out: "Did you tell me you loved me as I was finishing putting on my makeup?" My husband answered, astonished and embarrassed: "No, I never said that." My besotted brain must have mixed up "Let's go" and "Love you." There are periods when I hear him tell me he loves me several times a day.

Now this morning's yellow joy appears to me in its true form. It's not the yellow of the natural light of day. It's not the yellow of the sun and photosynthesis. It's the artificial light of an electric lamp. It's the yellow of lies, of adultery and hypocrisy. How could I have let myself be so foolishly blinded?

I take out the notebook that I remembered to bring with me. I was floating on a cloud this morning, but I must have already anticipated just how precarious my happiness was, now that I'm so used to sudden changes in the romantic weather of my relationship. A line with my ballpoint pen, and immediately I know what I have to do. I reread the text that I've left unanswered for two days, then write: "Yes, I'll be there, 5:30."

Then I take out my second notebook, the green one, the one that's not filled with solutions to survive the harm my husband inflicts on me but with advice and inspirational phrases about love: *stay mysterious, give him space, play hard to get.* The lists and quotes I've underlined in red give me the necessary courage to go to this meeting.

My lipstick (a cherry color from a luxury brand I chose for its name, Soulmate) and my heels that click unabashedly against the ground give me a new confidence as I leave school. On my way out, I remember with a wince that the day I met my husband was a Thursday. I wish I'd met him on a Monday (my favorite day) or a Friday (my lucky day), because meeting on a Thursday immediately subjected us to that ambiguous color: I met my sun and that day will forever be a happy memory; at the same time, yellow carried with it from the very beginning the warning of a potential betrayal.

When I arrive just after 5:30 (I have no scruples about being late when I'm not meeting my husband), Maxime is already waiting inside. Despite the warm weather, he is avoiding the terrace, where he could be seen (he's also married). I sit down opposite him. And then there's nothing more for me to do, as Maxime takes care of everything: signals to the waiter that we're ready to order, keeps the conversation going, compliments me on my skirt, asks me if I want another drink when I finish mine. He puts on a show. Is this how I seem to my husband? That I'm trying too hard? His attempt at seduction is clumsy. It's clear that he's attracted to me. Why doesn't he pretend otherwise? Why not act more aloof? Has he not learned anything either?

Despite his efforts, I can't muster any interest in him.

My husband thinks I'm at a faculty meeting, so I have at least three hours, which risks feeling very long if I have to listen to Maxime talk the whole time. I can't help but compare him with my husband. My husband would never have brought up our children in such terms. Unlike Maxime, he doesn't say "the little one" or "the older one," but always calls them by their first name after clarifying that our son is the eldest. My husband would never have ordered an espresso at this hour, and he hates short-sleeved shirts, even in summer. I can't help but pit them against each other: this man has nicer eyes, but my husband is taller. No matter what I do, my husband is my reference point, my measuring scale, my sea level.

I look Maxime straight in the eyes to avoid having to speak to him. I don't have much to say, and remaining silent at least makes me seem mysterious. And it's not a disagreeable sight; Maxime has nice eyes (honey mixed with green). His gaze struck me right away when I met him during a parent-teacher conference. He was one of the few fathers there.

I have only one desire: to drink a shot of tequila for courage. But I ordered a Perrier like him. Even sober, I can't chicken out now. I've been flirting with him over text for months. I've already accepted a drink, so I have to keep going; that's the rule I've set for myself. So I place my hand on his thigh.

My eyes riveted to him and my hand on his leg send

signals with consequences I can no longer control. Suddenly, I realize that this man's desire for me is so violent that he will not be satisfied with caresses on the knee or languishing stares. It's already too late. At this stage, he doesn't even want my mouth, even though he's never kissed it. A kiss would be an insufficient outcome for this game that has already gone on too long. So as we are speaking he puts his hand up my skirt, finds my underwear, and moves it aside to put a finger in me. I stiffen despite the evidence of my excitement seeping onto his fingers.

Maxime has booked a room in a hotel near the train station. When I enter, I automatically make a beeline for the window. I observe the passersby, the couples sitting on the terrace of the restaurant on the corner. Maxime wrests me from my daydream: "Why are you running to the window? Are you identifying the exits, like on an airplane? Are you already trying to flee? You know you can leave whenever you like, you don't have to do anything."

Under the sheets, the pressure of his hand on my arm takes me by surprise. Maxime doesn't push down, but he doesn't graze me either: I think he's . . . caressing me. My husband isn't very tactile. He doesn't like long embraces, and when people touch him it tends to make him uneasy. We obviously engage in physical contact—he holds my hand and kisses me on the forehead—but a prolonged stroke along my body to signal his tenderness? I'm not sure he's done something like that for many years, not since we began seeing each other. My husband makes love to me by putting me on all fours; I don't think he's caressed my arm in at least the last four years.

I shiver upon contact with Maxime's palm. I suspect things will go further (my body still holds the memory of his finger in me), but for now all he's doing is touching my shoulder, and I'm already picturing the most indecent acts. It's absurd, but it's true: just Maxime's hand on my arm seems more obscene to me than all the pornographic images on the Internet.

Sex with Maxime is a series of surprises. I am surprised by the way my clit melts under his tongue. I am surprised by his question when he puts on a condom and asks if I still want to. I am surprised by the shape of his penis in me, hard and pointed like a razor clam, almost cutting.

Intertwined, we roll around on the bed. The more we make love, the more I want him; that he's already inside me doesn't at all appease my desire—on the contrary, it arouses it. We climb on top of each other and grab at each other, and above all, we talk to each other. He whispers crude words in my ear. He says he loves seeing me get wet, come, groan. He loves my breasts and my ass. His vulgarity puts me at ease. I don't have to make love like a bourgeoise—he is not at all bourgeois. He reminds me of the boys from my neighborhood that I slept with as a teenager.

Maxime is not disgusted by my desire, by my fluids, by my groans, by my lewd words in response to his. He leaves my body to bury his tongue between my legs, then in my mouth; then it's his fingers, then his tongue again; then his penis is in my mouth. I didn't know that you could mix everything together like that, inverse the order. He tells me that the vision of my perfectly manicured nails on his penis excites him. That and my massive diamond ring, I imagine.

His nose is buried in my neck while he's inside me, his hand under my head. It takes me several minutes to realize that his hand is there to protect me. I'm on my back, Maxime is on top of me, and the top of my skull now grazes the edge of the wooden night table connected to the bed. Maxime placed his hand there so that I wouldn't bang my head. I'm overwhelmed with emotion.

I burst into tears. Tears that I don't recognize, that don't correspond with any category I'm familiar with. These are neither tears red with rage nor translucent tears of sadness. These tears are like a cascade, the breaking of one of those immense dams in South America that I've never seen. I'm crying for a continent where I've never set foot.

Apologizing, Maxime runs to the bathroom for a tissue and hands it to me. After a few minutes, I manage to articulate clumsily: "You put your hand on my head so that I wouldn't hurt myself." Maxime doesn't know what to say, his penis dangling between his legs. Faced with my flood of tears, he thought he was witnessing the sudden remorse of a married woman, or a total panic attack. He doesn't understand how a hand placed on my head could elicit such distress. "I wasn't going to let you hit your head . . ."

He hands me a glass of water. As I drink, my tears stop, as though the only remedy could be more liquid to drown out my cascade of tears.

"You're a little oversensitive, huh?" he says finally, rubbing my back.

My muscles relax one by one, I regain my calm. After a few minutes, I lie upside down on the bed, my head by his feet.

"Join me at the North Pole?" I ask Maxime with a smile back on my face.

He laughs, grabs the two pillows, and lies down next to me after opening the window. The scene is serene: the late afternoon light shines on the bed, the trains approach and grow distant again with a regular sigh, the smell of rain wafts up to our floor. Maxime's hand is on my arm again (pornographic), the incredibly soft duvet against my skin. (What makes hotel sheets so soft? Is it the detergent they use in industrial quantities? Their enormous washing machines that boil everything at high temperatures? Their dryers that leave the sheets as warm as though they just came out of the oven?)

As the light caresses my face, I feel the desire to take a nap, lulled by the sound of the trains. Maxime gives me an incredible urge to sleep. Proof that there is nothing between us: when you're in love, you want to talk to each other, see each other, be together. But when you sleep, you renounce the other: to sleep is to stop loving a little bit. That's why I've always been angry when my husband falls asleep so quickly in my presence.

Maxime's fingers leave my arm to stroll along the edge of my breasts, around my belly button, between my thighs. I start to touch him in return, but he stops me, grabbing my wrist. "Don't move. Let me." He asks for only one thing: that I look at him while he touches me. I stare into his eyes for another few moments, then I take refuge in his neck when I'm too close to coming. I'm afraid the orgasm will escape, that it will slip between his fingers, so I tell him to keep going, harder, faster. When I start to moan, he orders me: "Do it, come." It's the first time someone has said something like that to me. (Is having an orgasm really something we can demand of someone? Apparently yes. In any case, it worked.) I come under his fingers, my head buried in the pillow. This time, he hasn't even slid my underwear down my legs.

As I hook my bra, Maxime calls to me softly:

"Do you know that you have a mole on your lower back?"

He continues, hesitant:

"I'm not a doctor, but you should have it checked out by someone, it's a funny color, almost purple."

I'm mortified. Maxime must think no one ever sees my back. He must think that my husband doesn't make love to me anymore. He must think I'm one of those married women whose husbands haven't touched them in months. He must think that that's why I'm in this hotel room with him. He takes a photo with his phone to show me. The mark is in fact a strange color. I thank him and assure him I'll go see a doctor. Then I delete the photo from his phone (we're committing adultery, after all). I find myself face-to-face with a photo of his wife. I apologize for this invasion of his privacy—I didn't intend to see it, I didn't realize that deleting the photo from his phone would automatically show me the one before it. Maxime blushes and feels like he has to confirm what I didn't have the courage to say aloud:

"That's Clémence, my wife."

His wife is very beautiful (so one can be unfaithful even to a very beautiful wife—all the more reason to worry about my own marriage). They are on the terrace of a restaurant; his wife is wearing a pretty yellow dress and smiling at the camera, a glass of red wine in her hand. My husband has no photos of me on his phone, so I have a hard time imagining the scene: What sequence of random events could have led to the existence of this photo? What happened that night between Maxime and his wife? They've just finished their meal, they're waiting for the dessert menu, and suddenly he thinks to himself: "My wife looks so beautiful tonight that I absolutely must immortalize this moment. I want to preserve the memory of this smile and this light for all eternity"? Or maybe she suggested he take a photo to send to their family WhatsApp group? Or to a couple of friends who recommended the Italian restaurant downtown, as a cheeky thank-you? But no, Clémence's smile is intimate, her head slightly tilted, she's gazing tenderly at her husband: the photo doesn't seem meant for anyone but him. It also doesn't look like she's just come from the hairdresser, so she wouldn't be asking him to take the photo to show off her new color to a friend. It's nothing like that. I think Maxime must have spontaneously photographed his wife, just because he wanted to.

While Maxime is in the shower, I grab his phone: How many photos does he have of his wife? Photos of specifically her, without their children, taken of his own initiative on his phone when they're alone together with no purpose other than to preserve a memory. But his phone is locked and I don't have the code. After three unsuccessful attempts, it's blocked. I say a few words to Maxime through the bathroom door before leaving.

I exit the hotel feeling lighter. I had a good time, even if I know it wasn't for real, as the kids say. It was nice, but it doesn't count. The hookup will not be fruitful or productive: no child, no marriage, no ring will come from this afternoon spent with Maxime. Even the photo of my back, the sole souvenir of this moment, has been deleted. Nothing remains of the two of us.

It's the sad conclusion I arrive at each time. I often try to take a lover. These rendezvous have only one aim: to ease the romantic pressure that weighs entirely on my husband by dividing it among several people.

That's why I never feel guilty for being unfaithful: How could I, when I do it out of love for my husband? Plus, I know how to set limits: I've never cheated on my husband on any day but Thursday. It's not the color of betrayal for nothing.

So I flirt over text, I agree to meet, I wear a pretty dress, I get waxed, I let myself be penetrated a few times. But I would be better off facing facts: despite my best efforts, I've never managed to develop feelings for a stranger. I am truly incapable of having a real affair.

On the way home, I drive so fast that I almost crash into another car at a red light. Once parked in the driveway, I'm in such a rush to enter the house that I arrive on the doorstep out of breath. When my husband finally appears, I am happy to see him, even happier than normal. I never miss him so much as when I spend time with another man. My infidelity has the inverse effect of what I intend: I return even more in love with him.

Unsurprisingly, my husband asks me neither where I was nor with whom. Does he trust me or is he taunting me? I tell him about my faculty meeting in great detail, even though he doesn't ask me a single question. I justify myself, but he's not listening. He cuts me off to ask if we have baking powder somewhere.

The bulge of his penis through his pants is the only meal I crave tonight. Maxime merely whetted my appetite. I hope my husband will want to make love once the children are asleep. But I don't let it show because I know it might scare him off. My libido intimidates him. He must always be the one to make the first move. Masculine desire is fragile.

I watch my husband undress before taking his shower: he's wearing a piqué cotton sweater with a round neckline, a blue, slim-fitting Oxford shirt, beige chinos, microfiber underwear, lisle socks. I know all his clothing by heart. I could recite the labels with my eyes closed. I know where and in what circumstances he bought them—in what store, on what trip, for what occasion. I know which shirt he won't wear this week because the collar is stained. This certainty reassures me: I am on familiar, already-conquered terrain. The intimacy of a couple lies in the clothing. There is nothing more unsettling than running into a former partner and not recognizing certain parts of their outfit. (I know those shoes and pants, but when did he buy that hat?)

Sweater, shirt, pants, underwear, socks: my husband layers his clothing as though adding to his mystery. That's why he's even more handsome when it's cold out. He's not a summer man. I prefer when he appears thicker, when his cheeks are reddened by the cold, his lips chapped, and his hands gloved. He is at his most beautiful when bundled up.

My husband is irresistible in his navy-blue wool sweaters, much more so than when he wears shorts, sunglasses, or a bathing suit on the beach. And each winter, my husband is more handsome than he was the previous winter. It was only after I met him that I understood what it meant for someone to describe a man as "aging well" (or is it just my warped enamored gaze?).

Right now, he is less handsome than he is in the middle of winter, but obviously I'm still attracted to him. After all, I met him in August, and it didn't take me until Christmas to fall in love. But I ask myself often what would have happened if I had met him in winter: Would I have dared to make the first move? Wouldn't I have found him too attractive for me? If I had met him for the first time on December 10 and not August 27, would I have deemed him out of my league?

The winter doesn't suit me as well. I disappear under scarves and coats that are unflattering for my silhouette. On the other hand, the sun does me good. My skin is softer, the dresses I wear show off my legs, and suntan lotion pairs well with my natural scent. The seasonality of our looks doesn't match (provoking the question: Are we too different to be happy together?).

I listen discreetly to my husband from the other side of the bathroom door to see if he's singing a French song (which is what he does when he's in a good mood and more likely to want to make love). Then I pretend to read

The Lover as I wait, taking care to open the book toward the end (will he be impressed that I've read it so quickly?). A few moments later, my husband enters the bedroom. He's naked, he has an erection. It quickly becomes clear that the next fifteen minutes won't be spent commenting on my reading progress or debating the *nouveau roman*.

He doesn't undress me—he never does. Instead he asks me to take off my clothes. I obey, then he enters me. I let him. I'm past the age of giving blow jobs. And we're past the age of complicated experimentation.

He's quite hard, but his entire body is tensed against mine like a long wooden plank. I feel his penis pressing against me. I concentrate on his breath to gauge his pleasure. He uses his hands to impose a rhythm. I think again of the outline of his penis through his pants in the kitchen earlier. I desire him as though I've never touched him.

My husband still smells like sweat even though he's just come out of the shower. That lingering odor means he rushed through his shower to join me. He was so impatient to have me that he didn't take the time to wash himself thoroughly. Several years ago, when we had just come home from a tennis match, my husband wanted to take a shower before making love to me, but I felt bold enough to reveal that the smell of his sweat excited me, and he entered me on the spot. Perhaps he remembered that night? His thoughtfulness touches me.

Colors and landscapes flit by beneath my eyelids.

When I make love to him, I don't see fluids and bodies colliding, I don't see semen and I don't see a cock: I see concepts and colors, geometric forms and places. Tonight, the images alternate among a wild stream, lush greenery, steep cliffs, a humid tropical forest.

I restrain my breathing, I restrain myself. I put my fingers in my mouth so as not to moan. My husband probably thinks I'm trying not to wake up the children (fortunately the layout of our house facilitates our sex life, with the kids' rooms on the top floor). But in reality, I'm afraid that my desire for him will seem monstrous. I'm afraid that my excitement will disgust him if I come too hard.

I'm on top of him when I notice the small wad of tissue paper that's hidden beneath the mattress poking out slightly. I manage to slide it under the bed with the tips of my fingers without him noticing. Three rose petals, a pinch of coarse salt, a red ribbon: the age-old recipe for a love potion to prolong desire. I don't know if I believe in such things, but we have a rosebush in the garden, so why not use it?

My husband grabs my breasts and pulls me to him, which surprises me because he's never been particularly enamored with my chest. In any event, I've never understood what he desires. More precisely, I've never understood what he finds erotic—which details, which scents, which scenarios, which lingerie, which fantasies. After fifteen years together, I still don't know whether my husband is more of a breast or butt man. Tonight, my husband seems more excited than usual, but I couldn't tell you why.

Did he have a sex dream last night (which would explain his nocturnal words of love, even if he didn't remember upon waking)? Is it the effect of a low-cut neckline he glimpsed in a meeting this afternoon, or a coworker's inappropriate confession? Did he meet a mistress during his lunch break? Did he do things with her that we've never done together? Did he find in another bed what he no longer seeks out in our marriage? Is that why he is suddenly so fiery? Or has he just left his mistress? Are all his thrusts communicating his despair at no longer being able to touch her? Another possibility: Is it a sort of virile instinct awakened by the smell of Maxime on my skin? I've noticed that my husband always makes love to me on days when I've slept with another man.

I bury my nose in his neck to sniff out the scent of another woman. There's nothing. My husband has no mistress. And deep down, I know it. But even when he's deep inside me, my husband is out of my reach. Even now, I still miss him so much. When he leaves my body, he leaves a gaping wound, a horrible void, a gash waiting to be infected.

Friday.

Sitting in the breakfast nook, I analyze the geography of our bodies. I realize that I lean toward my husband when he speaks to me. It's my body that moves, not his: I change position, I inch closer, I twist my neck. My husband keeps his back straight and looks ahead of him when he eats, while I am lopsided and unbalanced.

I'm struck by this when we stand up to get more coffee: my husband's chair is perfectly centered. Mine, on the other hand, is turned to the left, toward my husband's.

I am convinced that if I made a map of my daily micro-movements, it would reveal that my husband is the sun around which the majority of my movements gravitate. I greet him at the front door when he comes home at night, I sit next to him on the sofa, I go to him when he speaks to me from the kitchen and I'm in the living room. I change rooms for him. Because of him, I am always the last to leave the table. I turn off the lights, I follow him up the stairs, I move behind him, remaining in his shadow. My husband, on the other hand, is not influenced by my comings and goings. My gravitational force is never sufficiently powerful to make him deviate from his course.

What physical forces decide our movement through space? What determines our speed and our strength? What is the physical formula? When I meet Lucie on Saturday mornings for tennis, our bodies meet halfway. I enter the club and see her seated in a chair near the entrance; she spots me, stands up, and heads toward me as I am walking toward her. We meet in the middle of the lobby, which seems to be a perfectly reasonable way of going about things. Why are the laws of physics that govern my movements with Lucie different from those with my husband?

My children eat in silence, their gazes still sleepy and their pajamas wrinkled. The only sound is that of spoons and bowls, the regular clangs composing an agitating music. I watch as they eat their toast and whisper a few words to each other. Their chairs are so close they might as well be glued together.

I've always hated children who talk too loudly. The decibel level that is socially acceptable for children has always seemed excessive to me. Under the pretext that they're children, that their voices are not yet fully formed, they are allowed to speak more loudly than adults. But I've succeeded at one thing at least in my children's education: they both speak very softly. Even when they were little, my house never overflowed with screams.

My husband informs me that he plans to swim after work tonight, then he has a dinner with a former co-worker who's passing through town. I am cold, impassive (I won't reveal that I'm bothered), but I grab my phone—like a life preserver in the middle of a shipwreck—which I have once more left on the kitchen table. I promised to stop, but I have a harder and harder time sticking to my resolution, especially when my husband cruelly announces to me that he won't be spending the evening at home.

Fortunately, today's breakfast is calm, so I can listen attentively to my husband's announcements (the pool, the dinner). I concentrate on his words so that I will feel less of a need to replay them later, to re-create the entire scene.

In our bedroom, my husband's clothes are on the floor in a corner. His towel, still damp, is on the bed. I gather it and hang it up. I don't comment on all his things lying everywhere. I also don't say anything about the mess in the bathroom, or the breakfast table he didn't clear, his dinners in town, his nights at the pool. Never any reproach of this kind. I refuse to succumb to such conventional arguments.

Actually, we don't argue much at all. Maybe that's what we're missing. And yet I adore conflict—broken dishes, slammed doors. I've always found tranquil partnerships uninteresting. Couples that don't ever argue come off as inferior, and I've always suspected they love each other less. But I've also always refused to engage in ordinary squabbles. That my husband doesn't do the dishes after dinner or doesn't know how to iron a shirt is annoying, but those are obstacles I can overcome; on the other hand, I don't know that I would be able to bear such a banal argument for such a trivial reason. If we argue, it must at least be a matter of jealousy or profound doubt, existential drama and painful soul-searching. I think it's essential that a couple's arguments always be about love.

I half-listen to the radio while wiping down the breakfast table, but I have a hard time waking up. I am still in the unreal state that persists when I emerge from sleep too quickly and my dream superimposes itself onto the day.

I dreamed again that my husband was a knight and I was his betrothed. My husband faced a series of challenges before he could reach me: sword battles, dragons, duels, horse races, poetry contests, dangerous precipices.

The events of the dream are always the same. My husband overcomes every obstacle in his path. He fights his competitors successfully; he's an unmatched knight and an unrivaled courtier. However, each victory triggers the beginning of the next trial. He continues relentlessly, succeeding at all of them, but ends up dying of exhaustion—a prisoner in a perpetual romantic tournament.

Except that, for the first time, my dream didn't end that way. Last night, my husband survived. Once he understood that there was no possible victory, that it was a trap, he forfeited and left. I don't love this dream, but it's a recurring dream, and a recurring dream is not supposed to change.

I serve myself another cup of coffee. My dream dissipates, and the pervasive feeling that accompanies it loses in intensity until it disappears completely, making room for Friday.

Friday is not ideal for concentration. It feels like a little vacation each week, a day volatile as a gas and comforting as homemade mashed potatoes. It's difficult to work on a Friday, even when I'm in the thick of a manuscript. If only I could find a satisfying translation for the title of the novel! *Waiting for the Day to Come* . . .

Fortunately, Friday brings me good luck because of its color: green. It's not just a superstition—there's real evidence to back this up. Whenever I've really needed it, I've looked for green around me, in a nearby object or in a landscape. If I find it, I know that things will end well. The day when I gave birth to my son, I was terrified. My husband met me at the hospital wearing a green T-shirt, and the birth went smoothly. When we first visited the house that would become ours, the green shutters confirmed that we were making the right decision. When we had an appointment to sign the paperwork for our house, the notary's green door, which I noticed only upon leaving, would have reassured me that my husband was already inside. I had a happy childhood, and I'm convinced that it's in part thanks to my mother's green eyes. Green can sometimes reach me in an indirect way, too: the night when I met my husband, the English band playing was called the Green Peas.

I look out the window. The lawn looks extra green today because of the dew, this omnipresent green that brings me luck more than any other color. Maybe there's a scientific explanation? After some research on the Internet, I discover that its place on the color spectrum corresponds to the wavelength 525 nanometers. Of course. I grew up at number 52 on rue Victor-Basch and I was born in Doubs, department 25. 525. Sometimes the best explanations are the most rational ones.

I've always seen days by their color. It's how I locate my-self in time. When I have a meeting somewhere, I rarely need to write it down: my schedule appears before my eyes in the form of a colored grid.

When I was little, I thought it was the same for every-one; I figured that the nuances of colors might have been different for some people, but that each person had their own mental rainbow. When I was in primary school I realized, rather painfully actually, that this was not the case. I said "yellow" instead of "Thursday" when referring to the school trip I was awaiting impatiently. The teacher laughed at my mistake, and when she corrected me, I tried to explain that, in any case, it was the same thing; I was convinced that Thursday was yellow for everyone. Laughs broke out among the rows of desks. I was humiliated when the teacher told me in front of the whole class that mixing up colors and days of the week at seven years old was no laughing matter: Did I want to go back to my little friends in kindergarten? Taking my attempt at explanation for insolence, she reprimanded me. For weeks, my classmates called me a witch and a liar and said that I was strange.

It wasn't until much later that I realized this colored perception of time also influenced my sight. It took me a long time to figure out, even though certain clues should have made it obvious: the tint of a lipstick would seem sultry and sensual on a Thursday night, but bland and insipid on a Sunday morning; there are certain dresses

I wear only on Wednesday, others only on Friday. On Tuesday, the day that corresponds to black, I am more sensitive to shadows and chiaroscuro (it feels like living in a Caravaggio painting, and I seriously wonder whether the Italian artist painted all his canvases on a Tuesday). And then there was that exhibition dedicated to the painter David Hockney ten years ago. In awe, I went back again the next day. But the paintings seemed different to me than they had the day before. I still liked them, but something had changed. I had such a hard time believing my eyes that I went to ask at the front desk whether they had changed the lighting that day. That was when I understood.

Now I know that, on Monday, blue objects appear with more intensity in my field of vision, and on Wednesday it's orange things. Tuesday, I searched high and low for my yellow notebook, the one containing the scientific vocabulary for my translations, in vain. Thursday, I found the notebook on the entryway table: no surprise, it took until the yellow day for that yellow object to appear. It's as though each day of the week places a filter in front of my eyes—a film roll with its own grain, or a certain sensitivity to light. Each morning, my entire landscape shifts in hue.

I've been working for several hours on my translation and am concentrating on one of the chapters when the title appears to me suddenly. The wait, the movement, the imminence, the dawn, the ellipsis, the poetry. It checks all the boxes. *Waiting for the Day to Come . . . En attendant le jour qui paraîtra bientôt.*

"Five Signs He's Cheating on You," "Three Things That Will Drive Him Wild," "Ten Secrets of Lasting Relationships": I stop at the articles with promising titles. I can't concentrate on my translation any longer, so might as well make good use of the rest of my day. And since Friday is the day of Venus, the goddess of love, I dedicate a part of my afternoon to my online romantic education.

I pay to access articles behind a paywall. I attentively watch several videos, peruse the lists of advice and exercises in women's magazines. An online quiz tells me that my marriage is in danger and that I must act fast to get it back on track. I retain a few salient lessons: give my husband a lot of space, be distant to cultivate mystery, make him jealous, don't confess what I feel so as not to smother him, don't burden him with an excess of emotion and sentimentality, and above all, don't let myself go physically.

What comes up most often is the necessity of mystery: don't reveal or say everything. The key words are "coldness," "inaccessibility," and "distance." It's easier for me to be absent now that the kids are older. But most of the time, I still need to be at home. Normally, I don't have any choice but to be present and available: I am in front of the gate to fetch the kids at school, in their rooms to check their homework, in the kitchen to prepare the meals, in our bed asleep, at my in-laws' house on Sunday afternoon, on the phone to ask whether I'm picking up the kids at the conservatory or if my husband will take care of it. The truth is that I am easily accessible. I'm told to act mysterious, but for obvious logistical reasons, it's very difficult to do so when you're married with two kids.

Of course, I diversify my sources: women's magazines, psychology, statistical studies, astrology, astronomy, political philosophy, personal development, fashion, cognitive science, history, decoration, sociology, gardening, anthropology, geography . . . I'm interested in everything that might be useful to my love life.

The green notebook full of romance tips is not my only notebook. I have several that I rely on, and each has its own purpose. A few years ago, for example, I started keeping a music notebook. The music my husband listens to gives me real insight to his state of mind, so I decided to meticulously record all of that data. For example, when he hums a French tune, that means he's in a good mood;

listening to a French song is also correlated to his sexual arousal. Brazilian music means he's calm, at peace. On the other hand, when he listens to pop, it's rarely a good sign: he becomes cold and distant, and the lyrics are often personal attacks.

Keeping these notebooks reassures me and helps me stay in control. I consult my notebook on romantic advice in moments of doubt. Before my date with Maxime yesterday, the inspirational quotes about lasting love gave me the courage to meet him. I knew I was cheating on my husband for the right reasons (having a lover makes me even more inaccessible and mysterious).

Of course, this notebook is also a painful reminder of my status as an eternal novice, as well as an admission of failure. Making a list of rules to follow so that the man who shares my life stays in love with me is rather sad. Why am I condemned to the inexperience of first relationships at forty years old?

When it comes to love, I've learned nothing. I've been reliving the same scenario ever since I was a teenager: I love too intensely and I'm consumed by my own love (analysis, jealousy, doubt)—so much so that when I'm in love, I always end up slightly extinguished and saddened. When I love, I become harsh, serious, intolerant. A heavy shadow settles over my relationships. I love and want to be loved with so much gravitas that it quickly becomes exhausting (for me, for the other person). It's always an unhappy kind of love.

Adrien, Antoine, Arnaud: my desire to love has always been so great that for each person I'm with, I love with the same intensity. To console myself over one, I leap into the arms of the next, incapable of being alone. Only my dependency on love, rather than on one or the other of these men, was a constant.

My inexhaustible need for love has elicited opposite reactions in each of them. For some, it was perceived as an excessive but reassuring proof of attachment. For others, it was a frightening and guilt-ridden responsibility. But in all of these cases, the relationships failed. So when I met my husband, real husband material, I decided to show nothing of my dependency. I had just turned twenty-five and I couldn't allow myself to ruin anything by stating my intentions too openly (to find the love of my life). Today I've learned to hide it, to pretend, but deep down there is still only one thing capable of getting me out of bed at any hour of the day or night: love. I've never managed to get any other hobbies.

This pattern of romantic desperation has condemned me to mix love with tears. I couldn't even escape it on my wedding day. I had to hide in the vineyard and cry in the middle of the party. The music and lights of the dance floor rapidly gave way to silence and darkness. Beneath my fingers were seeds of translucent green grapes. My mother must have seen me leave the party, because suddenly she was behind me. She didn't seem surprised by the two translucent tears on my cheeks, perhaps because it is socially acceptable for a bride to cry on her wedding day (too much joy, one hopes). But her words were unexpected:

"Love brings you sadness, just like your mother," she murmured to me, taking me in her arms with all the tenderness in the world.

Married just a few hours, my love for my husband was already painful, and I was learning, like Phaedra, that this pain might be hereditary.

Standing on a chair, I reach for the hair products hidden at the top of our closet and out of my husband's sight. In a shoebox, there's a brightening mask, products for color-treated hair, a shampoo with chamomile for blond hair. Staying blond when you're born with brown hair demands a certain investment.

When I met my husband, I was platinum blond. I had lightened my hair at the beginning of the summer, and the sun and the sea had accentuated my new color. When my husband went to order a drink at the bar, the friend who was there with him approached me and said: "He's crazy about blonds, you're exactly his type!"

In fact, I discovered later that all his ex-girlfriends were blond, with the exception of a Spanish woman with olive skin (her hair color kept me up at night for weeks: Did it mean that he loved her more than the others?).

Ever since, I've had to maintain my blond with bright-ening products that I hide so my husband doesn't suspect anything. I also don't tell him when I go to the hairdresser for highlights or a root touch-up. I don't know if my husband is aware of my natural color. When I renewed my passport nine years ago, I checked the box for blond.

I apply the product that's supposed to make my color last longer (if only it was so easy to make a relationship last). I let it do its work as I pace around the house. I wait. I wait for the product to take effect. I wait for it to finally be time to go check the mail.

I start by emptying my jewelry box and opening the false bottom. Inside: my mailbox key and my first engagement ring. An enormous fake diamond, gleaming and powerful, that I bought myself for 19 euros and 99 centimes on my twenty-second birthday. I'd been dying to have one for months. A whim, an idiosyncrasy perhaps. Is it so bad to pretend to be married? I reassured myself by saying that it was a harmless quirk: I wasn't hurting anyone. It's not illegal to wear a diamond on your ring finger.

My idiosyncrasy can be explained, though. At the time, I wanted my life to take shape. I wanted it to trans-form into something durable, firm. Like clay that dries and becomes less and less malleable, I, too, wanted to dry and harden. I was twenty-two years old and starting to grow impatient. I watched my friends' lives stabilize while mine remained uncertain—unreliable friendships, undecided career (teach? Start a graduate degree in English literature?), frequent changes in clothing style (my closet as witness). And above all, I hadn't found the love of my life—and there was no candidate on the horizon who was likely to be serious husband material.

To practice patience as I waited for my life to take shape, I gifted myself this ring. I wore it to buy groceries or to go on a run. Its effect was immediate. My intuition was thus justified: paying at the register and sweating at the park did in fact take on a new dimension with the ring on my finger. Suddenly, the most thankless tasks become more bearable. I can't explain it, but my faked status as a married woman finally showed the world that my existence had value. The transformation took place in the gaze of others: people assumed I was expected somewhere, that I had better things to be doing. Of course, I didn't wear it in places where I might run into a potential husband.

Three years later, I met my husband. Two years after that, he gave me a real diamond when he proposed, and I was able to say goodbye to my fake diamond. He knew I wanted a cathedral-cut diamond; there was no room for error. And so my current ring uncannily resembles the ring I bought myself out of impatience. I've kept it in the false bottom of my jewelry box ever since, and I take it out sometimes with a bit of nostalgia. I contemplate it thoughtfully, turning it in the light: pretty for a fake, but I prefer the real thing.

3:00 p.m. The quietest time in the neighborhood. The neighbors who return home for lunch have already gone back to work. It's too early for an office worker to be back, even on a Friday. Those who leave for the weekend are already gone: loading the cars for country homes happens just before 2:00.

The street is empty. I take the key out of its hiding spot, cross the yard, furtively open the mailbox. I inspect the contents with the tips of my fingers: nothing of concern (taxes, insurance, bank). Then I close it again, leaving the pile of letters as I found it.

No one saw me. I was right to wait. Monday, I wasn't careful and went a half hour too early, and a neighbor saw me. I take such incidents very seriously: I have to stick to the same rituals. Not respecting the rules that I've set for myself is a seemingly harmless error, but one that could compromise me one day. Monday night at the dinner table, my husband informed me that he'd found the mailbox open. I was petrified, but I covered my tracks:

"You're so absent-minded, it wouldn't surprise me if you forgot to close it on Saturday," I responded.

"Yes, you're right," my husband agreed.

I got away with it this time.

I'm not supposed to have a mailbox key. Things are organized in such a way that I have no need for one. My husband gets the mail when he comes home from work. He walks in with both hands full, envelopes in one and a baguette in the other, which always keeps me from hugging him.

For years, I was the one who got the mail. I lent him the key three years ago. I had to leave for the entire month of July while he stayed at the house. I didn't ask for it back upon my return, and that's how the silent transition took place.

Last year, the zeal with which my husband opened and closed the mailbox suddenly started to torture me: Why did he insist on getting the mail? How did he, so absent-minded, never forget to do it? He didn't have an answer. For months, I wondered whether my husband was writing to another woman, or if he was receiving anonymous letters—someone who knew about a former affair or an illegitimate child and was trying to blackmail him. That would explain why, when I suggested to my husband that we make another copy of the key, he simply shrugged his shoulders and replied that it wasn't necessary.

So then I was forced to implement an efficient but fastidious strategy. I claimed that I lost my keys one

day when my husband was out. I went to his parents'
house to grab their set, which also had a key to the mailbox. I made a copy that I keep hidden in my jewelry box.
I mentioned to my husband on the phone that I'd borrowed
his parents' keys and told him I eventually found my own
under the car seat. He didn't seem to suspect anything.
Perhaps he forgot that their set also had the mailbox key.
Since then, I've checked the mail every day and I'm far
less anxious: no blackmailer in sight, no impassioned love
letters to speak of.

Back in the house, I start with his bag. Then I move to his pants pockets. I unfold all the crumpled receipts. I read the hour, date, place, amount. Unfortunately, these details tell me nothing because I am not rigorous enough to piece the information together: I can't remember whether the lunches and outings he told me about earlier in the week coincide with these receipts. So I simply verify that he hasn't gone to a town he didn't mention or spend an unusually large amount of money.

I stumble upon a receipt from the cheese shop downtown dated last Sunday. My husband spent 73 euros and 23 centimes. A significant amount, more than the previous week. The more he spends, the more loved I feel. Crème fraîche and milk, eggs for his omelettes, Comté for me, sheep's milk cheese for the children, fresh goat cheese for our salads, Roquefort that I used in a sauce yesterday: enough to last more than a week. Ten days at least. A nice haul. The receipt of a patriarch (including the favorite cheeses of each family member). The receipt of a man who doesn't keep track of his spending (I imagine he crumpled the piece of paper nonchalantly before sliding it into his pants pocket as he left the cheese shop, not even looking at the amount). Above all, the receipt of a man who loves his wife and is not planning to leave her next week, since he bought enough cheese for ten days.

I finish with his computer. He hasn't changed the password for years. It's always what I do last, because it's what I most hate doing. Reading his emails makes my stomach churn. I know that my marriage might not survive the next message.

Now I can access all the contents of his phone from his computer—everything is connected to a single account, which saves me a lot of time. I skim his messages to his family and friends, things pertaining to his private life. But I scour the messages sent to other women or people likely to serve as alibis: Zoé, our babysitter; Maud, our daughter's piano teacher; Sylvie, the mother of our son's best friend; Damien, his coworker in the Milan office; Serge, his swimming friend. I also glance at the most recent addresses in his GPS: no hotels in the countryside or romantic restaurants with a panoramic view.

Everything is fine. I take a breath. Each week, I continue to worry. However, I have to admit that in fifteen years of life together I've never discovered anything of note: no site for extramarital encounters in his search history, no sex worker's number in his contact list. No mistresses or inappropriate messages with my closest friends.

On the other hand, I have found overly familiar exchanges, messages addressed to women with unfamiliar names. In the best-case scenario, I get to the bottom of it a few weeks later when my husband brings it up on his own: the wife of a friend, a former coworker, an acquaintance interested in a job at his company.

A few months ago, I came across an email exchange with a certain Éléonore in which she suggested a quick phone call. I was sure of it: they wanted to speak on the phone so as to leave no paper trail. I felt sick for days. Then one night he said casually over dinner: "You know, I've been talking to Éléonore, Valentin's wife—remember her? She called me because she's organizing a surprise birthday party for his fiftieth. She wants me to reach out to his former coworkers from the Oslo team. Nice, isn't it? The party is in February, hopefully not the same night as your publisher's party. It's the fifteenth, a Saturday night. Can you check?"

Of course, I wish my husband kept a diary: I would only have to read one thing to find out his deepest thoughts, and I could stop going through all the rest. The amount of time it would save me!

The major problem that arises from this ritual is that I am never surprised. My husband has never been able to plan something without me knowing about it first. Today, for example, I saw a receipt for two flights to Venice at the beginning of August. Now I have to wait for him to tell me and feign surprise. But I'm a little annoyed because I would have preferred to go back to Rome. I check the reservation details: the tickets are still refundable for another month. So I just have to drop subtle hints that I've been dying to see the Colosseum again, or remind him that we've never been to the Vatican. To broach the topic, maybe I'll suggest that we watch *Roman Holiday*, one of my favorite movies, together.

As I peruse the email from the airline (tickets aren't cheap this time of year, my husband must really love me), I wonder if he hesitated before making the reservation. Did he have to think to remember my birthday? Or did he type it in the form as automatically as his own? I got myself into quite the predicament with our birth dates a few years ago. I was supposed to spend a week in New York with my editor to meet the author of the crime novels I was going to translate. I applied for a visa, a simple formality. However, I almost wasn't able to leave because I had put my husband's birth date on the application instead of my own. I wasn't even shocked at my mix-up. It's exactly the kind of mistake I would make.

Sometimes I ask myself whether I should feel guilty about going through my husband's things. But I always come to the conclusion that I should not, for one simple reason: I wish he would do the same. I would finally have the proof of his jealousy and the confirmation of his commitment. Unfortunately, I know he doesn't. Unfortunately, my husband trusts me.

He has never read the love letter that describes an all-consuming adulterous passion in crude detail. I wrote it with the sole aim of checking whether he goes through my things. I've left it in various places throughout the house—under my scarves in the dresser drawer, in a shoebox in the entryway, in a wicker basket under my bedside table, in the largest book in the library—but my husband has never found it. Or rather: he's never bothered to look. Even when I left it out on my desk (it doesn't get more obvious than that), he didn't touch it. I know because I left a hair between the pages, and closed the envelope in such a way as to know with a glance whether my husband opened it (I discreetly folded the edges).

Alas, my husband is not curious about me. This realization is so painful each time that I've had to set myself a limit: I check the letter only once per week, on Tuesday.

If one day my husband were to finally read the letter, I know what I would say to him. I've already written the script. He would be wild with jealousy (a spectacle I dream of witnessing, even if only once in my life) and I would retort in an amused tone that it's not my letter. That yes, I wrote it, but it's an excerpt from a translation of the correspondence of a seventeenth-century English poet to her lover; I would explain that my editor was thinking of publishing it and asked me to complete a translation sample before finding out that the rights weren't available. I would show him the original correspondence in the library and we would laugh about his mistake. It would be incredible.

But my husband doesn't care what I might be hiding. He's never suspected that I see other men. I don't delete any of the messages I receive, nor do I take a shower to erase the smell of their bodies on mine. I know that I wouldn't lie if my husband asked me, looking me straight in the eyes: "Were you with another man this afternoon?" But he never asks any questions. I've sprinkled clues, and he picks up on nothing. I've left *The Lover* by Marguerite Duras out on the coffee table since Monday, but I'm sure he's not worried about it. I'm sure he's never asked himself: Why is my wife suddenly reading a book about a torrid love affair? I so wish I could glimpse worry on his face, interrupt his tranquil serenity. I wish distress or doubt would sneak in. But nothing. Sadly, I see nothing but confidence in his eyes.

I've always known that being in love takes time. In general, it doesn't bother me, especially not on Friday. (The day of Venus is made for this.) I have one last time-consuming task to complete, and it's far from the least: the recordings.

My headphones in my ears, I listen again to our conversation from this morning. I recorded it with my cell phone placed on the breakfast table. (What's the use of being able to record things on your phone if not this? I'm sure everyone does it.) The sound of the children's spoons and bowls keeps me from hearing everything. Fortunately they whisper at the table, otherwise a good number of my recordings would be completely inaudible.

I listen for my husband's evasive responses, concentrate on his word choices when he announces he's going swimming after work and then has dinner plans. He starts by saying that he has a meeting with "a former coworker" who's in town. Then, later on in the conversation, he mentions "coworkers"—plural this time. I go back to compare the two mentions.

I'll have to wait for my husband to tell me about his night, probably tomorrow morning, and listen closely: Will he mention one former coworker or several? I listen again to our conversations the way I analyze a text before translating it, with the same rigor: What is the tone? Why did he use this word instead of another? What was the author trying to say? What is the importance of this image, this comparison, this innuendo? Being a good wife may not be easy for me, but I can at least be a good analyst. I want to be certain that I haven't misinterpreted, that my besotted brain hasn't distorted his words.

Recording our private conversations seems perfectly reasonable to me: these words were meant for me, why shouldn't I be able to listen to them again? But it's a habit that costs me a lot of time, with not very compelling results. I often tell myself I'm going to stop, but I have a hard time cutting myself off. I try to pay more attention during our conversations (like this morning at the breakfast table, but I didn't succeed). I tell myself that my world will not crumble if our conversations aren't recorded. But knowing that I can listen to those moments again reassures me. Tuesday, I didn't record our dinner at Louise and Nicolas's, and I regret it: being able to go back to the precise moment when my husband turned me into a clementine would surely have helped me to see things more clearly.

I have exceeded the limit I've set myself only once. By chance, I had managed to record one of our rare fights, a conflict that destabilized me for several days. I transcribed it onto my computer, then translated it into English, being careful to cut out any identifying information. I printed out the text, then gave it to my students, telling them it was a chapter from an old English textbook, and that a conjugal spat would give us the perfect framework to practice the imperative. I was so desperate for a new perspective that I asked them for their opinion on the conversation. One of the students raised their hand and said, "The husband doesn't love the wife." A stab to the heart. I had to sit down for a second to catch my breath.

It's the only time I've used my recordings in class, and I am the first to admit that it was not smart. Most of the time, I settle for changing a character's first name to my husband's. This works well; my husband's name is very common in the Anglophone world. I even did it on Monday. What a delight to hear and pronounce his name for an hour straight. (I'm not hurting anyone, so why deprive myself of these small, simple pleasures?)

I go outside for some air, with my final goal for the day in mind: find the perfect lamp. I broke the old one on the floor on purpose; I couldn't let it ruin another night with my husband. (Why is it that something is bearable for months or years, and then one morning we wake up unable to stand it for a second longer?) We need a mellow ambience to preserve the romantic atmosphere of our living room. I'm convinced that the intensity of the lighting has played a part in distancing my husband from me on the sofa recently. Put the most beautiful woman in the world in bad lighting and her beauty will be noticeably diminished. I've always said it: beauty is a matter of lighting (15%), makeup (20%), hair (25%), and clothing and shoes (40%).

In the store, I pay attention to another detail. The switch needs to be high on the cord because my husband sits to the right of the sofa, and I sit on the left, next to the lamp; ideally, he would need to get right up against me to turn off the light. I find the lamp that corresponds to all of the criteria. And it happens to be pretty, too.

Waiting for my husband, I have a hazy night. Its contours blur like a pencil drawing that's been overly blended, or a watercolor drowned in too much liquid. The hours go by but lack definition.

My husband has told me that the state of singlemind-edness and concentration that swimming requires helps him to think. Underwater, free from distractions, he reflects on his daily concerns: a complicated case at work, a difficult client, his parents' ailing health. He emerges from the pool serene, each of his problems solved, his vision clear. Suddenly I picture him between two breast-strokes, realizing that his marriage is a mistake and a failure, that he feels like a prisoner in our house, that having children is a burden, that he's lost his freedom and renounced his dreams, that I'm not as interesting and cultured as his Spanish lover with the olive skin, that he doesn't love me anymore, that he desires another when he touches me, that he must and will leave me.

Or I imagine that he's never gone to the pool. Swimming is an ideal alibi: the perfect excuse to turn off his phone for an hour and take a shower to erase the scent of another woman. When he returns, I'll check whether his bathing suit is still wet in his bag.

Since the movie will be over soon, I leave the children in front of the TV while I wait for their father to return and I go to bed. From the bedroom, I hear his car in the driveway. I rush to turn off the light and glance at my phone: it's 9:58 p.m. By the time he locks the doors, finds his keys at the bottom of his bag, collects the mail, opens the door, it will be 10:00 p.m. My husband is punctual. So punctual, in fact, that sometimes I think he waits at the street corner for the exact time to come back home. Did he stay behind the wheel of his car alone for a few minutes? Did he turn off the engine and listen to one more song on the radio?

I hear his key turn in the lock and I can picture the scene. My husband in the entryway, the mail in one hand, his swimming bag over his shoulder, a relaxed smile on his lips. I think I hear two big kisses on the kids' foreheads. I imagine him sitting on the sofa to watch the last few minutes of the movie with them; maybe he's making fun of the villain, or letting them have another slice of cake even though they've already brushed their teeth.

The solid wood parquet floor creaks and the stairs groan, which means I always know where my husband is in the house. Our home seems to have been conceived by an architect who never wanted to be caught off guard.

Now I hear my children come up the stairs (since they go everywhere together, their steps resound with a single continuous noise). My husband closes the doors to their rooms, descends a floor, comes dangerously close to our room. I hold my breath; the door opens. I remain still under the covers. With all my strength, I pretend to be asleep. My husband lingers for a moment in the doorway and then leaves.

It's the last thing I'll do out of love for him today, on this day that I've consecrated entirely to our relationship: pretend to be asleep so that he doesn't see me with no makeup, in pajamas, my hair undone (he's made it clear that he doesn't like when I neglect my appearance). He will also miss me more in my absence, and we'll have more things to say to each other if he has to wait until tomorrow morning to speak to me. Play hard to get: I've learned my lesson. I wrote it down in my notebook just this afternoon.

Under the sheets, my body itches. No respite, not even on Friday. I try to concentrate on something other than my thighs and arms. I close my eyes and replay the film of our week. I stop at certain scenes, zoom in on interesting moments. I try to understand.

I don't reach any definitive conclusions, because everything depends on the level of magnification with which I observe and analyze our relationship. Everything depends on the romantic microscope.

On the scale of years, we share a beautiful love story. Over the course of fifteen years, there's been a marriage, a house, two children. Satisfying. On the scale of months, the landscape remains luminous: there is no month without a moment just for the two of us, without us making love, without tender words and a gift from him. On the scale of the week, the sky remains more or less clear: not a week without an affectionate gesture, a sweet remark, or a deep conversation. On the scale of the day or the hour, the romantic weather darkens. On this scale, I can detect all the ways he's distancing himself, all of his oversights. On this scale, I pick up on all the words he doesn't say and all the times he doesn't look me in the eyes.

But it's at the scale of the minute that the situation becomes unbearable. Let's take Wednesday night, for example. The children had gone to bed, and we were watching a movie on the sofa. My husband didn't take my hand even though I placed mine right on my thigh. Then I slid my hand under his. He didn't react. A few minutes later, he changed position, let go of my hand, and didn't reach for it again. When I zoom in on that minute, it's clear to me that my husband doesn't love me anymore and that our marriage is in great danger.

When my husband doesn't take my hand, when he turns me into a clementine, when he doesn't ask me about my day, when he closes the shutters and draws the curtains before going to bed, when he interrupts me, when he forgets the name of a coworker I tell him about often, when he doesn't seem particularly eager to see me again, when he lets go of my hand in the street, when he doesn't answer one of my calls, when I catch him with his eyes open during a kiss: those moments set my marriage to a sad soundtrack. Each moment adds a bitter taste of solitude, waiting, and abandonment to our fifteen years of love. And one moment can effortlessly cloud all of our years.

Saturday.

At first, it's a distant and muddled noise. Then gradually I start to identify the intonations of a voice. This morning, I am wrested from my sleep by my husband speaking to me from the bathroom.

He often talks to me in the same way whether I'm asleep or awake. It's as though he doesn't distinguish between the two, as though his brain can't interpret the clear signals: eyes closed, lying down, immobile, breathing deeply, no response to his questions.

He recounts his night to me. I hear the word "coworker" but don't grasp whether it's singular or plural. And, unfortunately, this morning I'm not recording.

My husband opened the curtains a little while ago, and the sun is blinding. He's already made breakfast and woken up the children. Now he's getting dressed in the bedroom. He's in a good mood and very chatty. Saturday is his favorite day. I know, because it's the day he talks to me the most.

Saturday is red. And my husband's Saturday—bright red. For him, Saturday is always a joyous event. It's no surprise he loves it so much; it's a day of leisure, to be spent outside, among friends. It's the first day of the weekend, and you're supposed to take full advantage of it: organize an activity for the kids, plan a night out with another couple or with friends. I prefer the routine of weekdays. Saturday intimidates me. It's a day that has to be reinvented each week, without even the Sunday rituals to cling to. Not to mention the social pressure of Saturday night: it's impossible to admit that you'd rather just stay at home with your husband, nestled against him on the sofa. There have to be dinners, invitations, outings, reservations. On top of it, today is our daughter's birthday, so we have to host a small party. (At what age does that stop being necessary?)

Saturday is the day I like the least and my husband likes the most. I'm sure I've ruined many of his Saturdays just as he's ruined many of my Mondays. If only our favorite days coincided—our life would surely be easier to plan.

I tie my hair up before taking a scalding shower (my preferred temperature). My husband joins me in the bathroom as I'm undressing, but my nudity doesn't faze him. He doesn't look at my breasts or my ass. After how many times seeing the same person naked do we stop being excited by it? When does the magic wear off? Six months, three years, ten years? Why does the 36,000th time we see a person naked not produce the same effect as the very first time?

My husband is sitting on the floor, his back against the bathtub. He likes to talk to me when I take a shower, through the curtain, like in a convent parlor or a prison visiting room. He vents the difficulties of his workweek. I learn that on Wednesday, a coworker in his department was fired. They weren't particularly close, but he was shocked by the way it was announced to the rest of the team.

I tend to forget he does this, but my husband often tells me important news after the fact. As if he needs to digest the information himself before communicating it to me, like a true introvert. This slight lag sometimes makes me feel like we're living in different time zones.

While he lists the doubts, disappointments, and joys of his week, he flips through the magazines wavy with humidity lying on the bathroom floor—magazines we leave there precisely for this purpose, when my husband sits near the bathtub to offer me a retrospective of his week through the shower curtain. When I turn off the water, he stands up to hand me a towel.

While I'm sitting quietly at the breakfast table, my husband suddenly suggests that we go to the cinema this evening. We could call Zoé to watch the kids and go see the movie he mentioned last week. Surprised, I drop my toast on the floor. I wipe the strawberry jam with a sponge; it looks like coagulated blood on the white tile.

I try to think of an excuse to say no. I've read the reviews: it's a movie about a separation, a man leading a double life and a marriage that's falling apart. I don't want my husband to expose himself to portrayals of unfaithful men. I know I can't stop him from coming across this kind of image or story, but when it's within my power, I'd prefer to avoid it. For example, I'll never give him a novel about such a thing, even if every Christmas and birthday, I'm faced with the fact that all the new books contain themes of adultery and marital trouble. (Why can't writers tell the story of a husband and wife who love each other with an overwhelming passion? Is a loving marriage not suitable material for a novel?) When we take my car, I turn off the car stereo so that my husband doesn't hear the new song by that musician with the blue eyes I listen to on repeat, whose catchy lyrics are unfortunately all about his lifesaving breakup.

MY HUSBAND

I tell my husband we have a long day ahead of us, which is true. Organizing a birthday party for our daughter seems daunting enough; there's no need to pile things on. Let's hope the movie won't be showing anymore by next weekend.

When I arrive at the tennis club, Lucie is already there. As she approaches me (we meet halfway), I'm about to compliment her on her hair (she's clearly just gone to the hairdresser). But I remember what happened when I praised Louise's dress on Tuesday night; I won't make that mistake again. And I went to the hairdresser this week, too—why doesn't Lucie say anything to me? Why should it always be me debasing myself with my considerate comments?

Exercising increases my heart rate, which I enjoy, because for once my husband has nothing to do with it. I like physical activity, but I don't try to push myself. Lucie is a bad sport, and I don't mind losing. I always let her win at the last minute. I accept losing as though failure were a part of me: I submit to it. I'm not aggressive at all, and I'm fine with that. I have no need to dominate in order to feel alive.

After our match, we grab a coffee in the club's café, which has a view of the courts. I talk about my husband, my children, my students, our summer vacation plans; Lucie tells me about Pierre, her daughter, her promotion, the construction on their country home.

"Did you hear about Marion?"

News of Marion, Lucie's sister, immediately wrests me from my torpor (the conversation wasn't particularly stimulating). Marion is forty, like me. She's a literature professor at the university, writes books about courtly love, gets invited on the radio to speak about medieval poetry. She's been married twice and has no children. She's a very beautiful woman (lovely hands, long eyelashes, magnetic charm), but above all, she's the person you hope to be seated next to at a dinner: she lights up when she speaks, she always seems to have stories to tell, her laugh can be heard from the kitchen. I've met Marion only two or three times, but I hear about her often through Lucie, who frequently complains about her elder sister's over-the-top behavior. Last year, Marion showed up at her house in tears—she was wearing a wedding dress covered in dirt, and her eyes were smeared with black makeup. Marion had been left at the altar, like in the movies: at a secret wedding with four witnesses, the husband-to-be had changed his mind an hour before the ceremony and fled to England with his young PhD student. Lucie told me the story, exasperated by the perpetual drama of her sister's life. I was struck by that scene. I imagined Marion in a wedding dress in the metro, barefoot, her heels in her hands, crying, hair undone, eyes rimmed with mascara: what a fantastic, sublime image.

Now Lucie tells me that her sister is back to being madly in love with her second husband.

"But it won't last. I'm just waiting for the next catastrophe," she adds.

"Why are you such a pessimist? Is Marion doomed to be unhappy?"

"I'm convinced of one thing. My sister is so obsessed with love because it helps her avoid thinking about real problems. Love is a distraction! It's so much simpler to cry on Monday over her first husband, whom she says she'll love the rest of her life, and then get back together with her second husband on Wednesday, after a fleeting infatuation with a man she met on a train the week before . . . It's easier to cry over a man than to think about the cancer she's been battling for ten years, or the fact that she won't ever be able to have a child."

Fascinated, I listen to Lucie speak about love as a distraction and wonder whether I have some of Marion in me.

I want to continue the conversation: Why does Marion experience love so intensely and why do her relationships always seem destined for failure? Why does her heart beat stronger than the other hearts around her? But Lucie makes it clear that she'd rather change the subject. It's obvious because she's blushing—her emotions visible on her cheeks like two signposts. How does she manage to maintain any mystery with Pierre if her cheeks betray her?

That's when I grasp something essential about Lucie, an aspect of her personality that had escaped me up until now. I had a hunch, but I couldn't put my finger on it: Lucie is a prude. I have finally found her third existential word. Lucie is precise, opinionated, and prudish.

When I'm not too absorbed in my own thoughts (which center on my husband to a worrying degree—it's difficult to quantify, but I'd say approximately 65 percent), I play a game that can last months, even years. I ask myself how I might describe one of my friends or family members in three words. It's less an attempt at description and more of a real existential quest: find the three words that encapsulate who a person *is* to a tee, what makes them *them* and no one else. For example, I've figured out that Louise is whimsical, loud, and frank, and that Nicolas is elegant, restrained, and thoughtful—but it took me a long time to settle on each of these terms. (The first of the three existential words for Louise is not

"funny," "playful," "comical," "witty," or "amusing"—
it's "whimsical.") I've also started listing the three words
in order of importance: the first is the least significant,
and the third is the one that most closely captures the
mystery of their personality (for Louise, of course it's that
she's frank).

The exercise is dizzying, because even two people
who greatly resemble each other at first glance (socially,
personality-wise) do not ever share the three same existential words. For example, all the men I've loved correspond
to the same type, and yet they have no word in common.
Adrien was affectionate, egotistical, and insecure. Antoine
was prideful, disillusioned, and an aesthete. Arnaud was
passionate, humanistic, and creative.

It took me four years to find my husband's three existential words, to feel that with three adjectives I could
sum him up without any blind spots. My husband is
charismatic, introverted, and contradictory. He also has
a great sense of humor and is gifted with extraordinary
generosity, but that doesn't count: it is not what makes
my husband who he is. He would be the same person
without his humor or without his generosity, but not
without his charisma, his introversion, or, of course, his
contradictions.

His charisma was obvious even the first time we met.
The term "charisma" encompasses thousands of micro-
impressions that my husband sows everywhere he goes:

an aura, an assurance, an allure, a way of speaking and holding himself, an evident relaxation, a confidence in himself and his own good looks. He captivates. He attracts. He draws you in.

On the other hand, it took me much longer to land on his introversion, because my husband has many friends and likes to be surrounded by people. He's also not shy. But I came to understand that it's when he's alone that he recharges his batteries. To make an important decision or to digest an unexpected announcement, he needs solitude. In critical moments, he subtly turns inward. Whereas an extroverted person instinctively turns to others (as Louise does, for example), he withdraws (and evades me at the same time).

My husband is charismatic and introverted, but it's his contradictions that best characterize him. Of the three, this was the word that proved the most difficult, the part of him that escaped me the longest. But once I identified it, it was also the word that gave me the most satisfaction. I was finally certain that I really knew the man with whom I share a life.

Contradiction is the coexistence of two contrary and incompatible realities. My husband is full of them; he travels roads the wrong way, swims rivers against the current. He is both serene and profoundly anxious— and his serenity and anxiety coexist, equally real. He wants freedom but dreams of family life. He admires social success and the brilliant careers of the London finance world as much as he scorns them. He adores being around people but needs alone time. He strives to meet people and speak in public even though he hates being the center of attention. It's as though he's always struggling against his true nature.

Since he is never completely at ease with his own choices, my husband envies people who live the lives that he didn't choose for himself. The contradictions running through him create a breeding ground for jealousy. I even wondered for a while whether his third existential word should address his envious nature, but I confused the symptom and the cause. My husband's ambivalence regarding Nicolas is a good example. Nicolas's freedom, his first child at forty, his modern duplex downtown, his high-level finance job: my husband envies these things as much as he disdains them.

I once made the mistake of asking my husband what three words would best characterize me. He responded without much hesitation: very beautiful, cold, in love, observant.

"That's four!" I protested. "That's not the rule!" I reacted to the number so as not to reveal my distress over the words he chose. "In love with you? Of course I am! We are married, after all," I reprimanded, trying to appear unbothered.

"No, not in love with me, in love. In love with love," my husband corrected.

"I'm not in love with love! That would mean I love the idea of being in love more than I love you, which isn't true."

I defended myself tooth and nail, arguing vehemently, which made him smile:

"You're a little too defensive for there not to be some truth to it, don't you think?"

I hated that game.

My coffee with Lucie might be my favorite part of playing tennis in the morning. In any case it's the part I try to prolong. Because for the first time all week, it's my husband who's waiting for me and not the other way around. At noon, he's at home with the kids. Then it's the noise of my car door slamming, my steps that announce my return in the flowery driveway, the sound of my key in the lock: it's me who appears in the entryway as the meal is being prepared, my tennis bag over my shoulder. It's important that he wait for me for a change, so I create an opportunity by going to the court every Saturday and ordering a second coffee at the counter even when I don't really want it.

I don't particularly like tennis, and getting up to go

on Saturday mornings requires a certain effort. But I motivate myself, thinking it will be good for me to do something other than think about my husband (but do I ever stop?) and, above all, to leave his field of vision. For once, I will be inaccessible and busy. I can then reappear a few hours later, ever so slightly new (I've experienced something without him), body firm and showered (this is the way he likes my body the best).

Playing tennis, staying at school to grade homework, going to dinner with friends in town, pretending to be asleep when he gets home late at night: during these absences, I hope he misses me. However, I know that I lost the benefit of novelty long ago. He never looks at me anymore like I'm a stranger entering a bar or someone else's wife. I don't know if I'll ever understand why I've never stopped observing my husband from afar, with the necessary and sufficient distance to be able to admire him.

ortunately, it's only once per year and once per child. I might be a bad mother, but I don't think any parent in their right mind, even a very loving one, could find their child's birthday party tolerable. It's my personal definition of hell: noisy children at the center of attention, conversations between parents judging each other with as much discretion as the red dress I'm wearing today (in other words, none).

Curiously, it's not my plunging neckline but the strawberry shortcake on the table that is the object of everyone's attention. People ask if I made it. I noticed that several parents share this strange obsession: determining which mothers bake cakes themselves for their child's birthday. Is there a known link between being a good mother and being a good baker? I haven't read that in any article, though I have to admit that I take more notes on love than on parenting. In fact my husband made it, which earns me an approving look (a husband who bakes, *I'm so lucky*). It seems unnecessary to mention that he is also the one who tied balloons to the front door, hung colorful garlands in the trees, covered the sideboard with an animal-print tablecloth, and filled the large glass carafes with lemonade and ice. He also set up speakers in the yard for music. Everyone around me is praising all the things my husband has done for my daughter today; *I'm so lucky*, it seems. But being an excellent father does not automatically make you an excellent husband.

More and more children arrive. Some are my son's classmates (I discover that, even at school, my son and my daughter hang out in the same circles; in my memory, there was an insurmountable border between the little kids in second grade and the ones two years older in fourth grade). Everything is too red today. Too nervous. Too much noise, too much sun, too many requests. We don't have any more plastic cups, I'm told; my husband asks me to fetch a bottle of chilled white wine. Lucie calls to me: her daughter Anaïs stained her skirt with strawberry coulis—do I have something to clean it? Is there more lemonade in one of the fridges? Where is the bathroom? Would it be possible to have a glass of water? My son is allergic to nuts, are there any in the shortcake?

We take a photo with the four of us as my daughter blows out the candles (our family portrait will be perfect—

this day has not been a total waste). Then she unwraps her gifts: presents from her classmates, a gift from her brother (it's the first year my son has given something to his little sister; did my husband help him?), then from us. Eight presents to celebrate her eight years, including colorful sequins for dressing up, a book by an illustrator she likes, watercolor pencils. I see that my husband has wrapped them in eight different wrapping papers, creating a heap of colors, textures, and shapes, all different but charming together. I am moved and jealous at the same time. I can't remember the last time my husband made the effort to switch up the paper or the color of the label for each of my presents. For me, he plans weekends in Venice, nights in a hotel, romantic dinners, outings to the opera or the theater: certainly lovely and thoughtful, but nothing that keeps, and certainly nothing that comes in colorful wrapping paper. On top of it, he's never made me a cake or hung garlands in the trees for my birthday.

Today my daughter is sociable and sunny, even talkative (so she inherited her charisma from her father; I'm not sure that's a good thing). I don't understand: we never hear her say a word at home. Over the course of a conversation, I learn that she wants to become a veterinarian. Now I understand why so many of her classmates gave her animal-themed gifts and why my husband chose a tablecloth with an animal print. He seems to have been in the loop. I feel as though I've been gone for two years on vacation without them, or like I just woke up from a long coma. My own family eludes me.

I stop counting how many glasses of wine I've had. I shouldn't have had so much to drink in such a hostile environment. When I'm drunk I have a tendency to let my guard down. I'm afraid of tensing up conspicuously when my husband talks about me in the third person as I'm standing right next to him, or stiffening when he insists that I speak about my current translation project ("the bestselling novel of a young Irish writer that was adapted into a TV series, it's a huge opportunity. People can't wait for it here in France, isn't that right, sweetheart?"). I serve myself another glass of wine to keep from saying anything when my husband praises my translation work to the small circle that's formed around him, but forgets to mention that I'm also a high school teacher (a wife who teaches is a much less impressive trophy).

When I come out of the kitchen, I find my husband deep in conversation with Lucie. Shamelessly, he's devouring her with his eyes with as much fervor as though she were revealing the secrets of the universe (she's probably talking about the construction on their country house, and after being subjected to that conversation this morning I know there's nothing so exciting about it). They might as well be making love in the middle of the garden. I don't move. Lucie's two red cheeks give her away, it's written all over her face: my husband is flirting with her.

Then I lose all control. It's no longer my brain that's in charge, but my instincts. I see myself drag Pierre inside on the pretext of needing help in the kitchen. He follows me without seeming to understand, but without resisting either—we're going up the stairs and he knows that the kitchen is on the ground floor. I lock the door to the bathroom behind me and throw myself at him. My husband devoured his wife with his eyes, I'll devour her husband with my tongue. An eye for an eye, a tooth for a tooth.

Surprised at first, his mouth slowly responds to mine. He pulls my hair back, as though to resist for a moment, then gives in when I move my fingers to his pants. He has just enough time to say: "What are you doing?" I slide my underwear down my legs and guide him with my hand. When he enters me, he grabs my breasts with desperation, clinging on as though to two rocks on a cliff face. Everything disappears: the door against my ass, the bathroom where I shower every morning, my husband's close friend. I am transported to somewhere in the Alps, in the middle of a major climb, three hundred meters over a void. His crazed thrusts are dizzying. Is it the forbidden fruit of extramarital sex, or is Pierre just as brutal with Lucie? Does Pierre always make love as though he were going to die the next day?

It only lasts a minute or two, but it's enough time for me to realize what I've just done. What a foolish risk. Cheating on my husband around so many witnesses. And cheating on my husband on a Saturday, when I only do it on Thursdays. There are rules, they must be heeded, they're there to protect me. Why didn't I do what I always do? Lock it away, wait to be alone at night and take out my notebook to write down what wounded me? Take some time, distance myself. That's the rule: always wait until the next day before reacting.

I come out of the bathroom trembling and wet, and I make eye contact with my husband through the window. He's in the garden, a glass in his hand, and he's staring at me. He turns his head away, but I'm certain of it: his eyes locked on mine.

My panic is so intense that I feel like I'm drowning. Is it possible my husband saw me? Or did the window act like a two-way mirror—I saw him but he couldn't see me? Did he only catch sight of a silhouette, or did he see me come out of the bathroom followed by Pierre hurriedly adjusting his clothes?

I have to keep calm. Collect myself, remain rational, assess the parameters. My husband was in the garden. He must be fifteen meters from the house. I was on the second floor—a floor is three meters high, but since our ground floor is elevated, we're already five meters up, and I'm more than a meter from the ground, so let's round up to six. We form a right-angled triangle, 15 by 6 meters. Pythagoras, Pythagoras, Pythagoras . . . What is the formula again? The square of the length of the hypotenuse is equal to the sum of the squares of the lengths of the other two sides . . . 15 squared is 225 . . . 6 squared is 36 . . . 225 plus 36 equals 261. Now I have to find the root of 261 . . . 16 times 16 is 256, 17 times 17 is 289 . . . So that's it: between 16 and 17 meters. That's the distance between me and my husband. Not much, not much at all.

But how many glasses of wine has my husband had to drink? Four, five? He's not drunk, but has he had enough to blur his vision? 5:00, summer solstice, the sun is already to the west—I must have been backlit.

I stare at my reflection in the entryway mirror and command myself one last time to stay calm. I start by reapplying my lipstick, a tint slightly darker than what I normally wear, halfway between violet and maroon. Then I let down my blond hair so as not to have to redo my bun. It flows neatly down my back; my diligent brushing has saved me.

No matter what happens, act as though nothing is wrong. Stay in control. Even if my husband saw me, he'll think he was imagining things. He can't honestly think that his wife would sleep with another man at her daughter's birthday party. Improbability will be my best defense.

When I go back to the garden, Lucie asks me if everything is okay. She says I have a funny look on my face. It's true: I'm deep in my mental calculations (the root of 261 is not a whole number), and on top of that I just orgasmed (which makes my cheeks flush) and I can feel her husband's semen running down my legs. I wonder if anyone can see it.

The children have finally gone to bed. At the end of the table, I open a bottle of wine before approaching my husband with a smile and a glass in each hand. We're finally alone. And this time, the lighting is perfect. It was such a good idea to smash the old lamp on the floor and buy a new one yesterday.

I am relaxed, almost serene. My husband has no clue about Pierre. If he had seen me, he would have said something. "What were you doing in the bathroom earlier? I saw you come out with Pierre, is there something going on between you two?" But my husband doesn't ask me a thing.

Even so, I could have sworn that we locked eyes through the second-floor window. And seeing someone isn't the same as locking eyes. Locking eyes implies a reciprocity: it's active, it's reactive, it's instinctual. It's the predator staring down its prey, and then the prey lifts her eyes, suddenly aware of her fate. I must have imagined it.

My husband even appears to be in a joyful mood. Maybe I can hope for a declaration of love or a few tender words. All the days of my week are ruled by the sign of love, but I know that my husband loves me the most on Saturdays. So I have to take advantage.

My husband puts classical music on the living room speakers. This is a rare occurrence, and I wonder how to interpret it; my music notebook says nothing about classical music. I think it's Mozart—it's a well-known song. Of course, I don't ask him for confirmation. What would he think if he found out his wife wasn't able to recognize Symphony no. 40 in G Major by the most famous composer of all time? He knows I don't come from the same social and cultural milieu as him, but I've made so much effort to hide it that I think he often forgets—no use reminding him.

We've barely had our first sip of wine, the dramatic violin harmonies have just given way to the melancholic oboe (maybe it's Haydn? In any case it's after Bach, second half of the eighteenth century, that's for sure; the phrases are symmetrical and the harmonic language very simple), when I hear footsteps on the stairs. My daughter appears in the doorway. Is a night alone with my husband really so much to ask? We've already spent the whole day celebrating her birthday.

My daughter murmurs that she has a stomachache. She sits on my lap and then buries her face in my neck. My only thought is that she's going to ruin my makeup. The bronzer on my neckline and cheeks is spoiled now.

I'm a monster for thinking about my complexion while my daughter is trembling in my arms. I collect myself, stroke her hair, and squeeze her little body, warm as a croissant, against me. I signal to my husband that I'll take care of it and go up the stairs with her to her bedroom. I take her temperature and spend some time comforting her. I give her some medication that I dissolve in a glass of water (she doesn't like to swallow pills): if she's still not feeling well in an hour we'll call a doctor. Finally, I lie down with her and sing her favorite song, "Sunny."

It's been a long time since I've sung for her. I used to do it more when she was little, borrowing the words of others to show affection. She would ask me the meaning of the English words, again and again, even though she knew them by heart ("What does 'you're my spark' mean, Maman?").

When my daughter drifts off to sleep, I close her bedroom door gently behind me. Monstrous. Guilty. Even though I lingered, even though I think I've done what a good mother would have. Monstrous for thinking that this was time stolen from what should have been a night alone with my husband. Guilty for glancing at my watch.

I've barely walked out the door when I hear her call to me again. I freeze; I've already been quite patient. I go back, turn on her bedside lamp, kneel down next to her, and look her straight in the eyes—the gentle mom mask is gone. I grab her wrist and squeeze it tight to paralyze her little arm in my hand. And with bloodcurdling coldness, I hiss an order: "Go to sleep now."

But when I go back to the living room, it's already too late. My husband has finished his glass of wine. Our moment is over.

When my husband begins to close the bedroom shutters, it's the last straw. He has to lean out the window to grab the hook. For years, we've been saying we need to figure out another system: the hook is much too far away, we have to stand on tiptoe to reach it, it's dangerous. As I approach my husband and stand right behind him, breathing down his neck, I toy with the idea of pushing him. Would I have the strength to knock him over the window guard? If he grabbed on, would I be able to press down on his fingers until he let go and dropped into the void? I know that I would. There are no lights on in the house across the street, no compromising onlookers, no neighbors out late walking the dog. No risk. The decision is mine: Does my husband deserve to live? I have no difficulty picturing him unconscious on the ground, his skull fractured, blood flooding his brain.

I have even less difficulty picturing myself as the inconsolable widow (black looks good on blonds)—the woman who had everything before a freak accident permanently altered the course of her existence. I hesitate, renounce, retreat. Perhaps it's a disproportionate vengeance for being forced to sleep with the shutters closed. Instead, furious red tears spring from my eyes like two erupting volcanoes. Why can't he grant me a single concession?

Turning around, my husband finds me in tears at the edge of the bed (why doesn't he seem surprised?). He leans over me and asks what's wrong. I can't reasonably explain to him that sleeping in the dark is driving me insane, that since Monday I've been plotting my revenge against that structural injustice, thinking about his punishment. I can't tell him that I've just imagined murdering him while thinking about what I would wear for his funeral (I have a black dress from last season that would work quite well, but wouldn't it be a great opportunity to buy a new outfit?). I also can't tell him that I'm angry at myself for having been so reckless and slept with Pierre during our daughter's birthday party. And I can't confess that I'm still waiting for an explanation for the clementine, that I want to know once and for all why he decided that ridiculous fruit represents me. I can't even bring up the other night again, back him into a corner: Are you sure you didn't tell me that you love me in your sleep on Wednesday? How can you be so certain? Maybe you talk in your sleep without knowing it? What gives you the right to question the validity of my perception, especially since I wasn't the one asleep? And why didn't you hold my hand on the sofa on Tuesday night while we were watching TV?

Since I can't reasonably tell him the truth, I invent something else. I murmur: family, children, work, relationships, mixing real pain with the first complaints that come to mind. A confused stream that my husband can't make anything of, except that I wish we had more alone time. He answers that we'll be on vacation soon and we'll spend several weeks together.

I'm upset with myself for cracking in front of my husband. What was the point of exerting so much effort and playing the strong woman to then burst into tears on his favorite day? What was the point of carefully applying my makeup when my mascara is now running down my cheeks? And on top of it, since I cried, my husband will certainly not make love to me tonight. He never sleeps with me if he's seen me cry in the last twenty-four hours (do tears disgust him?).

Once I've calmed down, I venture to ask him to tell me about our day. I try not to do it too often. Sometimes he refuses, when he's tired or doesn't feel like it. But tonight, he kindly agrees to play along.

The idea is simple: he must describe our day for me, from his point of view, from breakfast till bed. He must put words to what we experienced together. I prefer his words to mine because I have more confidence in his interpretation of events; he is often more objective than me. And I've noticed that he has a tendency to erase from his narrative the hassles, the arguments, the yawns, and the sighs, which in my world often take up so much space that they eclipse the rest.

He recounts his morning: his good Saturday mood, his orange juice, his jog around the lake, breakfast with the kids, a story on the radio about a pet boar that made the three of them laugh, our conversation in the bathroom, going to the library with the children, where he ran into the parents of our son's classmate—his father is a lawyer, his mother a pilot, we have to invite them over for dinner one night—preparing for our daughter's party, his joy at seeing her so happy and surrounded by her friends, going to the grocery store, then to the chocolatier to buy me a bar with raspberry, driving back to the house, the radio program about the environmental crisis that gave him a lot to think about—Are we doing enough? What kind of world will our children grow up in?—the board game the four of us played after dinner, his tenderness at seeing our son be so sweet to his little sister, their bond, the pleasure of a glass of wine once the kids were in bed—he loves that wine that Pierre brings back from Bordeaux every year; speaking of Pierre, he thought he seemed strange this afternoon but he's not sure why—our daughter appearing in the doorway, the boring TV show, his sudden fatigue, bed, the watch I got him for his birthday that he's very careful with placed on the bedside table, he wonders whether he might have damaged it yesterday, my tears of exhaustion, and finally me, turning to him on the pillow, calm again, he knows that look: I'm about to ask him to recount our day from his point of view.

I hang on to every word. Transported, I observe our world from the window opposite.

Then my husband asks me to undress. Once again, he makes love to me on a day when I've slept with another man (I'm starting to believe in the power of his masculine instinct). I'm thrilled. I would never have dared hope for such a thing: for one because I've just been crying, and also because we already made love on Thursday night. Once a week, very reasonable, is our average (I have all of our stats jotted down in a notebook somewhere, and we're about the same as the average in France). Once a week, that's respectable: not too much, not too little. Nothing to brag about to Nicolas during their nights out, but nothing to be embarrassed about either. At forty, once a week is normal. And that's what I want to be: normal.

Once he's finished, he kisses me and turns back to his side of the bed to fall asleep. I hate when he turns his back to me, but if this is how he sleeps best, can I really reproach him for it? Is a husband required to sleep facing his wife? How do other couples sleep?

Immediately, my body starts to itch. I can't sleep despite the taps I do on the inside of my wrist with my thumb and index finger. The questions that normally soothe me are ineffective tonight. Even the lullaby I made up is of no use:

Do not despair, do not despair
He's not going anywhere, not going anywhere
Tomorrow his love will still be there, still be there.

I think of my body, itching, and my husband's body, so close but now out of reach (dizzying to think that less than ten minutes ago he was inside me). I can tell by the rhythm of his breathing that he's not asleep. It's slightly too rapid; maybe he's pretending. But I'm sure: my husband is not asleep (if there's one thing I know, it's his sleep). I must be keeping him awake by not being able to sleep myself. He hears me tossing and turning, scratching, thinking (I don't believe he can really hear me think, but I know that a contemplative brain consumes energy; can my husband feel the heat of it?).

We've been lying in bed for over an hour now. I don't dare move anymore. My disparaging presence in the bed exhausts him. It's true that I have many complaints about his sleep: Does he really need complete darkness? Why does he turn his back to me? Couldn't we fall asleep spooning? Why is it always so easy for him to fall asleep after a difficult day, when it takes me hours?

Suddenly, he turns around and leans over me. I startle and then freeze. His face is right next to mine, he moves his hand toward me. Time slows, almost stops. My husband will grab my neck and squeeze it tight. He'll clamp down until I can't breathe. He's sick of listening to me think and feeling my eyes on him. He knows that I record our conversations and listen to them on my phone. He knows about Pierre. He feels spied on. He'll strangle me, mirroring his own suffocation. He wants to make me disappear. I will die between his fingers because he can't take it anymore. My husband hovers over me, advancing, his hand is on my neck. I won't fight back. I won't scream or resist.

My husband leans over my face and kisses me on the cheek:

"Can't sleep, sweetheart?"

Sunday.

Sunday morning begins peacefully: the Brazilian music, the toasting bread, the sunlight streaming in. The breakfast ritual unfurls smoothly. I don't know why, but I feel a particular tenderness for my children when they come down in their pajamas. My children ask me if I slept well, and I wonder if that shouldn't be the other way around.

And then my husband whispers those fateful words in my ear. "We need to find a moment to talk. It's important."

It is a small mercy that I have mastered a façade of cold, unfeeling beauty that allows me to seem unfazed. I take another sip of coffee to catch my breath.

I'm sure my heart skipped a beat. I read a very serious article on broken-heart syndrome. The Japanese have a word for it, *takotsubo*. In France, doctors call it *sidération myocardique*, "myocardial stunning": the heart stops due to intense sadness, then starts again. So I know that dying of heartbreak is not just for heroines of seventeenth-century novels. Discreetly, I move my hand to my chest: I feel the contraction of my heart behind my sternum, the valves and ventricles shut momentarily. Everything is fine.

My husband uttered that murderous phrase while leaning toward me, his hand on my lower back. Why did he put his hand on me? To ease the shock of the announcement with physical contact? Or is it a way of showing that what he has to say is important but not bad? That we have to find a moment to speak but I have no reason to worry? Or is he trying to act like everything's fine in front of the kids? Did he whisper those words to me in front of them because he was afraid of my reaction? It's cowardly to use them as a shield.

My husband resumes the conversation as though nothing happened. When he's finished with his coffee, he goes upstairs to take a shower while I stay seated at the breakfast table. I search for a green object nearby, anything at all in my field of vision that can assure me I have nothing to worry about. But I find nothing. My gaze stops at the kitchen clock, which is peacock blue: maybe I could call it dark green?

My children are talking to me, but I can't understand what they're saying. They seem to be speaking a distant and incomprehensible language that I can't decipher. Finally, I hear them ask: "Maman? Are you okay, Maman?"

I wish I could tell them no, that I'm not okay, that my husband is going to leave me tonight. Or I could say it in a way that would impress the urgency upon them: *your father* is going to leave me tonight, do you understand? We'll tell you next week after dinner, probably Wednesday night, when we've had the time to choose the right words and the right moment. We'll all be seated around this very table. My husband will get up to turn off the music, and then he'll come back, place a solemn hand on my shoulder, and sit down next to me. He'll be the one to speak first: "Kids, your mother and I have something important to tell you." He'll have a very adult way of phrasing things. He'll remind you that we love you very much and that our separation won't change that. He'll tell you that it's not your fault and that despite everything we'll remain a family.

This scene that I visualize effortlessly (I've imagined it so many times) unexpectedly puts me at ease. For all this time I haven't been crazy after all. My anxiety was founded, my fear legitimate all along. I had every reason in the world to be worried: my husband really did intend to leave me.

But this isn't my greatest fear. Yes, I'm afraid that he'll leave, that he'll ask for a divorce, that he'll cheat on me, that he's still enamored with his first love, that he'll fall for a coworker, that he'll come out as gay, that he'll lose all passion for me. The list of my fears is long, but there is one dizzying fear that surpasses all the rest. My greatest fear is that one day people will say about us: that man spent thirty-five years with a woman who wasn't the one.

The pain is relentless, an octopus that wraps around my neck and squeezes. Everything hurts and I can't hear anymore, but I am relieved. By leaving me, my husband is rectifying the situation, correcting course. He always makes good decisions, and he's often right (on his reading of Proust, on the best route to avoid traffic, on his geopolitical analyses of the Middle East). I have a blind confidence in his judgment: he's a good man and an excellent father. If he's leaving, it's because it's the right thing to do and the right moment to do it. I just have to let it happen. I don't need to stress or try to do anything about it. I can close my eyes, succumb, let him handle the situation. My husband knows what he is doing.

My relief mitigates my pain. It's the relief that comes when what we've been dreading finally happens. When we're playing hide-and-seek and our hiding place is discovered. When a loved one we cared for deeply who's been sick for a long time passes away. When the main character of a horror movie is caught by the monster who's been hunting them. It's a good thing. I have nothing left to fear, because what was bound to happen has happened. I have nothing left to fear, because *the worst* has happened.

I've been afraid that my husband was dying to divorce me but didn't have the courage to act on it. The more time passed, the less his presence in our bed each night assured me that he really wanted to be there. I knew that our marriage, our two kids, and our house forced him to be there with me. Paradoxically, I was more confident when we had just met. His love for me was purer then because nothing kept him by my side. Today, I wish I could yell it from the mountaintops, tell it to all the women expecting marriage to be the ultimate proof of love: marriage guarantees nothing, except that he won't tell you he's cheated with a coworker because he'll have too much to lose. Having children with the man you love is even worse: now he's forced to be with you for years even once desire has fizzled out.

When we have a boyfriend or girlfriend in kindergarten, the entire relationship plays out during recess. In middle school it's a week: Monday you're together, and by the last class on Friday it's over. In high school, maybe it's a month or two: you fall in love in September, everything is over by Halloween. Already the time before the breakup has gotten longer. In your twenties, separation can take an entire year, but if one of you lacks the courage, you can add two years more to the count. After forty, it takes at least ten years to separate. Ten years between the moment you realize it's not working anymore and the moment you decide to leave.

Luckily, my husband is not a coward. I've always admired his frankness; even if it no longer works in my favor, my husband is undeniably wonderful in that way. He won't put off what's right in front of him for another few years. He'll leave me abruptly, from one day to the next. This morning we woke up married, tomorrow we'll wake up separated. I feel sick at the idea that soon his mouth will be off limits to me, that I'll no longer have the right to kiss him, that I won't be able to refer to him as "my husband."

It's easy to identify a first time, but we rarely know when something is happening for the last time. How could I have guessed that it was our last carefree Monday? The last dinner with our friends? The last time he would make love to me? (If I had known, I would have imprinted in my body's memory each of his thrusts, his breath on my neck, the way he turned me over on the mattress.) And, on a larger scale, how could I have foreseen that it would be our last Christmas? The last of our daughter's birthdays celebrated together? Our last vacation? If we could identify our last times as easily as our first times, thousands of moments would be lived more intensely.

It's over. My marriage is crumbling, a failure (a breakup always is). Even so, I don't know whether I regret having chosen this relationship. Because at some point we all have a decision to make: choose to love or to be loved. There is no couple where love is shared equally; it's not possible. So we have to determine which kind of romantic life we'd like to lead: Will we be the one who receives or the one who gives?

Before meeting my husband, I lived several love stories. I was always loving desperately and intensely. There was only one exception: Adrien. For the first time in my life, I was with a man who loved me more than I loved him. Two years with Adrien, going to sleep before him every night; two years with no sadness but also with no passion. With my husband, I knew immediately that it would be the inverse, that the power dynamic would be to his advantage. So I hesitated. I even left him a few months into our relationship to give Adrien another chance. Two weeks of wavering, lulled by the sound of the waves. But in the end I chose my husband. Loving more seemed the more noble choice. And my attraction for him was so intense that I wondered sincerely what I would do if I couldn't see him every day for the rest of my life. His way of speaking, of walking through a room, of moving his hands: everything about him immediately overwhelmed me. Breathing the same air as him, sharing his bed, going on vacation with him: it was all a privilege that I couldn't turn down. Maybe my husband's charisma skewed my judgment. In any case, I left Adrien and the seaside, I renounced the comfort of being loved, and I went back to my husband for good.

Today, I don't know if I regret my choice, but I see that I paid a high price, much higher than I had anticipated. If I had chosen to be loved rather than to love, I would certainly have been a better mother. And I would have had the necessary headspace to form real friendships and focus on my career.

But why leave me this year? Why leave me in the spring? Why leave me today? Sunday is a strategic choice, because it's indisputably a white day. If the other days' colors are more difficult to decide on, Sunday is unanimously white. Of course, it's a sacred white. It's also a universal promise of peace: my husband can be assured that our separation will be peaceful. And he put on Brazilian music, which is what he listens to when he's calm and serene. So he is not tortured by his decision—he is sure of himself and will not go back on it. Everything will go smoothly.

But the white of Sunday is not as simple as it seems. Optics teaches us that white is the result of a combination of every color (and not the absence of color, as I once thought). It's not the purity of the bride or the emptiness of the blank page: Sunday is neither neutral nor naive. White is the synthesis of every color, just as Sunday is the synthesis of every day of the week. It's the final result, the last chapter, the solution.

My daughter sits at the piano. My son takes out his clarinet. They're practicing for the year-end concert at the conservatory. It's in three weeks and I already know the piece by heart. Imagine a long sorrowful moan, or a four-year-old child whining for seven minutes straight. (Poulenc is rarely festive, but this piano-clarinet duo is particularly dreadful.) If I hear it one more time, it will sap the last of my remaining strength. I'll go wash my hair to drown it out.

I stare at my reflection for a long time in the bathroom mirror. I don't recognize myself. Perhaps a shower will help me feel back to normal. I make the water colder and colder, turning the faucet until the frozen stream leaves a painful mark on my body. The cold anesthetizes me. It helps me submit to the white of Sunday. Particles of dust float through the air; I glimpse them in a ray of sun. My moisturizer is an immaculate white when I place a dollop on my hand (I hadn't noticed this brilliant white the other days of the week). The milk in the children's bowls also stood out with a particular gleam over breakfast. And of course I chose a white silk shirt. As I was standing in my underwear in front of the dresser, suddenly white appeared as the most comforting color, and the only one I could reasonably wear to get through this day.

White helps, but it doesn't stifle the questions racing through my mind. I learned not long ago that there are two ways of thinking: some people think in a long interior monologue with full sentences, while others reflect through abstract concepts. I belong to the first category, along with nearly 60 percent of the population. So in my head I ask myself: Why now? Why this morning? Why today?

Did my husband stop loving me a long time ago, but want to wait for the kids to be a certain age before telling me? Did he think that divorcing before the summer would be a good idea? This way we can move before summer vacation and the kids won't have to change schools during the year.

Even so I am astonished that he would leave me in June. The statistics on this subject are clear: divorces are more frequent after vacation than before (at the end of the summer and after Christmas). These facts are circled in red in my notebook of romantic tips. For years, sociologists and economists have observed that the divorce rate is not correlated to a rise in unemployment or the real estate market; on the other hand, at the end of each holiday, divorces systematically increase.

According to the latest data, the risk of divorce increases after five years of marriage. It makes no sense—we've been married for thirteen years (maybe it's because of that unlucky number?). With our separation in June and after thirteen years of marriage, we will be the exception that proves the rule. But there must be a reason why my husband is leaving me now. Did he see me on Thursday with Maxime? Did he catch me and Pierre yesterday? Did he meet someone else? Come to think of it, now it seems obvious: the plane tickets to Venice weren't for me. We've never gone together, we have no memories there: it's the ideal place to begin a new romance. He'll discover Doge's Palace with his new partner. He'll tell her that he loves her for the first time in front of Saint Mark's Basilica and they'll make love for hours in their hotel room with a view of the Grand Canal.

While I'm fastening my earrings (gold hoops given to me by my husband that I'll no longer be able to wear without crying), the truth appears to me suddenly, simple and chilling. My husband has no idea about Maxime or Pierre. He hasn't met anyone else; the tickets for Venice were for me. He's going to leave me because he found the notebook of punishments I've kept scrupulously for the last two years.

He must have come upon it while moving books around in the library. When he opened it, he would have been shocked to discover its contents, with my comments in the margins. This notebook is nothing like a diary: no long, pathetic complaints (like Phaedra, I hate pouring my heart out), no psychological analyses. Instead there are three columns drawn with a ruler: offense, punishment, date.

On the first pages of the notebook, I established the most frequent offenses and the corresponding punishments. For example, "forgetting to wish me good night before going to bed" means "no cuddles the next morning." Similarly, "staring for a long time or repeatedly at his phone on the living room sofa when I'm sitting right next to him (even if the TV is on)" incurs the following punishment: "not picking up the next time he calls (and not calling back until he's called at least twice)."

These are two punishments that I had to enforce at the beginning of this week, with the aim of reestablishing equilibrium between my husband's behavior and my own. That's the very principle of restorative justice—and I know from experience how important it is to be in a relationship with a baseline of equality.

To avoid arbitrariness, I opted for a codified system: for each romantic offense there is a punishment. It's as simple as that. My nine-year-old son learned in the first trimester of school that arbitrary power is an authority limited by no rule, exercised according to the will of a sovereign. It's out of the question for me to act on a whim or change my mind from one day to another, to be angry at my husband on Monday and tell myself that it wasn't that bad on Tuesday. The rules exist for a reason, they are always the same, and they must be followed.

When I enforce a punishment, I ignore the particular case or the extenuating circumstances. I don't seek excuses for my husband: I simply take the facts and obey the consequences. Whether he's tired, stressed, or sick, the same code applies. In court, the judge doesn't ask whether the accused comes from a modest family or whether he was having a bad day: for each crime there is a punishment. The fact that my husband's mother didn't hold him in her arms enough when he was little or that he had a difficult workweek must not be taken into consideration. It's hard, but it's the rule.

A crime: a punishment. Three hundred sixty-five days a year. That's the foundation of our modern criminal justice system, and it has proven its worth. Why shouldn't we apply it to the private sphere? Laws regulate our behavior and allow us to live together in society; it should be the same for domestic life. My husband knows that he must wish me good night every night, that he owes me respect and loyalty. There are weeks when I don't have to take out my notebook from its hiding place in the library. Weeks without punishment exist—it is possible.

This system is by no means cruel; quite the contrary. Its primary goal is to simplify my life. It limits the number of questions I have to ask myself each day: when my husband hurts me, whether his betrayal is serious (the clementine incident) or trivial (looking at his phone on the sofa), I know what I have to do (apply the corresponding punishment). I write down the offense with a ballpoint pen, and the solution appears to me. It limits my nights of anxiety, the wounds that fester and never heal, because from the moment my husband is punished, I feel that he's paid his debt. And then I can start to forgive him.

New crimes make a regular appearance in my notebook; despite the years, my husband still finds new ways to torture me. But sometimes it's also that it takes me some time to gauge the level of the injustices I endure. For example, the closed shutters in our bedroom every night. I never thought my husband should be punished for it, that his need to sleep in total darkness constituted an infraction. But my frustration began to grow, to take up more and more space, until my tears of rage erupted last night. I still haven't found the punishment capable of reestablishing balance, of making amends for my forty thousand hours of destructive sleep in the dark. Finding a punishment proportional to the transgression is the most difficult part: I can't be too severe (I won't push him out the window, even though I briefly toyed with the idea yesterday) nor too lax (refusing to kiss him in the morning is not sufficient). Perhaps a long-term punish-ment, like a poisoning? A small dose in his coffee each morning when I've had trouble sleeping because of the closed shutters? Of course, not enough to kill him (the pro-portionality of the crime and the punishment is the very foundation of justice), but a mild laxative or sleeping pill could do the trick.

It's not all so black and white. There are gray areas. For example, I hate when my husband goes to sleep with his back to me, but I don't think that constitutes an offense in and of itself. I don't appreciate it, but it's not against the rules—although to be sure, I would have to find out how other couples sleep.

This week was particularly intense. I don't think there was a single day without an offense or a punishment. Maxime was, of course, the most serious punishment. I've been flirting with him for months, but I was forced to follow through with it when my husband retracted his nighttime declaration of love. When his words hurt me this much, sleeping with another man is the pre-scribed punishment. It might seem severe, but it is in fact fair: denying someone's perception is just as violent as adultery. If my husband had confirmed his "I love yous," I never would have slept with Maxime. I would have instead taken advantage of the fake faculty meeting to go shopping. I would not have told my husband—he likes me to dress well but he finds the activity frivolous, so I update my wardrobe discreetly (though he does sometimes notice, like with the new dress I was wearing on Tuesday night at Louise and Nicolas's).

With Pierre yesterday, it was different. I completely lost control. Of course, I had to punish my husband for his misconduct with Lucie, but not in that way, not on the spot, not blind with rage. Before reacting, I always take the time to record my husband's transgression in my notebook and wait to punish him until the next day. Rarely do I act the same day. It is essential to take the passion out for the justice system to work. It limits excess: reacting in the heat of the moment like I did yesterday was reckless.

This week, I had to inflict other punishments on my husband, including: "pretend not to hear him when he speaks to me" and "move his things (wallet, keys, bag, clothes, important document)." These two punishments corresponded to the following two offenses: "withdrawing his hand from mine and not putting it back after" and "humiliation in front of witnesses (friends or family)." For this last one, I hid his wallet to cost him time as he was leaving for work.

Like every day, he had left it on the entryway table; all I had to do was put it in the pocket of the pants he wore the day before.

But given the gravity of the triple humiliation at Nicolas and Louise's (his unpleasant memories of our first month as young parents, my erasure from the story about the security alarm at his birthday party, and, of course, the clementine), I also decided to hide his folder containing important work documents. I knew that this way, I would not only cost him time, but I would also have to bring the documents to him.

I started moving his things years ago, long before the punishment notebook. One morning, I took his keys from his coat pocket while he was in the shower. Another time, I hid in the closet a package he was supposed to take to the post office and that he had left in the entryway so as not to forget it. A few months later, my husband went to see a doctor.

It came from good intentions. I had just gone back to work after our daughter was born, and there were entire weeks when my husband and I barely crossed paths: I would leave early in the morning, he would come back late at night. That's when I started to hide his things, so that he would ask me to bring them to him at work. We would meet near his office and have a coffee together before his next meeting. That's what I did on Wednesday with his folder, and I have absolutely no regrets. I created a very nice moment between the two of us—romantic memories don't fall from the sky, one of us has to fabricate them. Moreover, I like being the one who always knows where things are so I can help him out of compromising situations. It's a constant reminder that he needs me.

I started moving my husband's things because I missed him. I continued because he needed to be punished and because he deserved it.

My husband has found my notebook of punishments. He will never forgive me. How could he? If he had found my notebook of romance tips, or the inventory of his musical choices, I would be petrified with shame, but I could have claimed it was research for a translation. With this notebook, though, he'll confront me and I'll have no way to deny or downplay the facts.

My body trembles, I can't breathe. I'm hot, cold, afraid, hungry, tired. I need an excuse to go for a drive. I tell my husband that I finished the last pack of my birth control pills and have to go to the pharmacy.

I drive aimlessly, with only one thing in mind: the Supertramp CD in my glove compartment.

The first notes of the flute, then the saxophone, instantly bring me back to the 1980s, but this song feels perfect for this moment, as though it were written for me.

Composed for *this* drive, the soundtrack to the end of *my* marriage. In fact, I'm convinced that this song has been waiting for me in the glove compartment for years.

The keyboard comes in gently, almost timidly, beneath the saxophone. Then it fires up, takes the lead. Then come the drums, which add to the despair, and then the saxophone returns. And finally, the first words: *Don't leave me now.* No ambiguity: a lament. Pleading, direct.

I can't stop myself from translating at the same time as I sing (occupational hazard). *Ne me quitte pas maintenant. Ne me laisse pas dehors sous la pluie battante, dos au mur.* For the moment to be perfect, it would need to start raining, the windshield wipers would be moving frantically. But the song's "pouring rain" is missing and there's no chance of it falling with this hopelessly blue sky.

A driver stares at me as we stop at a red light. I'm singing at the top of my lungs, clearly devastated. He must be wondering whether I'm going to drive my car into a wall at the next bend in the road. The light turns green. Foot on the accelerator, eyes blurred with tears, I belt as loudly as I can. You have to admit, the song is effective. I'm already in a trance and the saxophone solo hasn't even begun. At the peak of my despair, I blow through a stop sign. If a police officer arrests me, hopefully my tear-smeared face will dissuade him from giving me a ticket.

Ne me quitte pas maintenant. Ne me laisse pas le cœur

vide. My heart is so full of my love for my husband. Will it stop beating if it loses its object? Will it still function with no driving force, no purpose?

The Supertramp song lasts 6 minutes and 25 seconds. It's long (the average song is 3 minutes and 49 seconds), but not long enough. I replay it, once, a second time. It's just as emotional as before. Then I dry my tears and find an open pharmacy. Before getting out of the car and entering the house, I powder my nose again.

I go through the motions for the rest of the day. We drive to the grocery store, we eat lunch at my husband's parents' house, the children bike around the lake, we drink coffee on our way back from our walk, I bite into a piece of chocolate filled with raspberry, I fasten a button on my husband's shirt, we eat dinner, we all play a board game together. But I'm not really present. I choose fruits and vegetables at random. I take the wrong exit at the roundabout on my way to my in-laws'. I'm almost hit by a car because I'm looking the wrong way on the road to the lake. I forget to drink my coffee, which ends up going cold on the kitchen counter. I bite my tongue so hard as I'm eating my chocolate that its taste mixes with that of the blood in my mouth. I prick myself several times with a needle to see if I'm still capable of feeling something. I burn myself on purpose as I cook the meal. I never know when it's my turn to play.

But I smile. I tell my husband that I'm tired, and it's true. I'm exhausted. The pressure, my doubts, the waiting: everything has come crashing down. All that remains is immense fatigue.

The children are finally asleep. My husband stayed in their bedroom a little longer than usual. Did he say a few words to prepare them for the change that's about to occur in our family? Did he read them a book meant to help children cope with separation, about parents who get divorced but continue to love their two children very much? Or did he recount the history of France like when they were little? Did he tell them about how Napoleon abandoned Joséphine for a younger woman?

I'm sitting on the bed, waiting. I hear the water running and I can barely breathe. I place my hand in front of my nose to check whether I'm still breathing. I don't know how to act. I'm not sure how to take in oxygen from the air as I inhale, nor how to emit carbon dioxide as I exhale.

My husband comes out of the shower. I emerge from my apnea. He's wearing the faded shirt he's used as a pajama shirt for years and his boxers with the ocean motifs. The irony. My husband will finally end our marriage while wearing a shirt for his favorite rugby team and ridiculous fish-patterned boxers.

I didn't think he would be cruel enough to end our fifteen years of shared life in our bedroom on a Sunday night like any other. I didn't think he would leave me while not wearing pants. But then again: Where else would he do it? It's not like he was going to invite me to dinner in town to ask for a divorce, or bring up separating between two games of tennis. Nor could I expect him to put on a suit to tell me he's met someone else.

My husband sits down next to me. He grabs both of my hands in his and makes a small compact ball (the gravity of the gesture consoles me a little).

We're at the edge of the bed. This is where we sit for our serious talks. Never again will we have these nightly conversations—these impromptu executive councils in which we decide on how to ask for the advance my editor still owes me or whether to buy a gaming console for our son. This conversation at the edge of the bed will be our last, but at least I'm aware of it, so it will be imbued with the rare beauty of an intentional last time.

I want to cut him off. Tell him that I know, that I'm ready, that I've been waiting for this moment for a long time. But I can't manage to make a single sound.

My husband is thinking, contemplating the right words. In everyday life, he speaks more freely. But when he has something important to say, he always takes his time. That's precisely what he's doing now. He concentrates, retreats slightly, gauges the distance, gathers the necessary energy, and finally takes the plunge:

"There's something I wanted to talk to you about. I don't know how to broach it, I've been thinking about it for a while now, maybe you've picked up on it. We're both turning forty this year, the children have grown up . . . They've grown up so fast. So I said to myself, it's now or never. What would you say to growing our family? A third child, what do you think?"

I hear myself answer yes, I see myself kiss him. I'm wild with joy. My husband loves me.

I have to stop rifling through his things, recording him, punishing him. I nestle against him, drunk with happiness over the ultimate proof of love he's just given me, and certain of the positive changes I'll put into effect starting tomorrow morning. That's what Mondays are for.

I close my eyes, cradled by my husband's oceanic breathing, and my thighs start to itch. I ignore the signal, I bury my face in the pillow, I twist the covers between my legs and refuse to scratch. But the itching spreads slowly to my head, my arms, my stomach.

Epilogue

This week, I was really on my game. Her notebook as witness. Everything is in there: even that I withdrew my hand from hers on the sofa and then rebuffed her three attempts to get it back. My little wife writes it all down. My darling. She gets herself so worked up.

My favorite part was waking up in the middle of the night to tell her that I loved her. She was beaming with joy the next day, until she called me in a panic a few hours later to demand confirmation. Of course, like every time, I denied it coolly.

She goes nuts when I do that.

It's incredible to think about, really: you should believe your own ears, I repeated it three times! Have more confidence in yourself, have some self-assurance. How can she doubt herself to such a degree? My wife's vulnerability is staggering: Just how far will I be able to go before she fights back? Will she ever put up the least resistance? Will she finally rebel one day?

I have to admit that I've pushed her to the limit the last few days: gawking at the pretty waitress at the Italian restaurant on Wednesday afternoon, going to sleep without saying good night right in the middle of a conversation, terrifying her by whispering that we have to talk. And I was not very kind when we were at Louise and Nicolas's. But to be honest, I didn't think she would get so upset over a clementine. I really thought the fruit suited her! It's deliciously sour, and you can devour a thousand in one sitting.

This week was particularly intense, but going off with Pierre during our daughter's birthday party, seriously? I was afraid someone might see them leaving the bathroom; it wasn't very smart, given that the hallway window looks out right onto the garden.

I'm not angry at her—I should have anticipated that flirting with her best friend so obviously right in front of her would send her spiraling. But like I do every time, I made love to her that very night. I do it systematically whenever she sleeps with another man. I mark my territory, and it's a way for me to communicate tacitly that I'm not angry at her, that I forgive her.

Next week, I'll behave impeccably. There'll be no writing in the notebook, not the slightest faux pas. Maybe

I'll even be a little overzealous: an impromptu declaration of love and a nice gift, why not. She must already know about Venice since she goes through all my emails—but that will do the trick.

The secret to keeping the scales of power tipped to my advantage is to switch up the intensity: if every week were like this one, she would be exhausted and numb to everything. So, after a particularly grueling week—a crescendo from Monday to Sunday—I have to ease up on her. That way she lets her guard down, puts things in perspective, remembering that she and I do have good moments. She even guilts herself: How could she have been so angry at me when I'm such a loving husband?

I need to establish serenity between us so I can set my latest strategy in motion. I found out about a new form of male contraception this week, which gave me the idea to suggest that we have a third child. It's a thermal and reversible method that's easy to conceal, thanks to which my wife will believe she's become sterile—or worse, menopausal. It will distress her for months, not being able to give me what I want—she will be eaten alive by worry that I'll leave her for a younger woman capable of giving me a child. I think I'll use the contraceptive method for a few months, and then when she's least expecting it, I'll get her pregnant. In any case, she'll love the child less if I get her pregnant right away—and we both know that motherhood is not her strong suit. Come to think of it, I'd love to have a third child with her. Seeing Nicolas and Louise so happy sparked my desire. I am a very present father—and I've always told myself that my softness compensates for her coldness.

My wife does not love motherhood, but she loves our children, and that's all that matters. I'm not complaining. I have so many friends whose relationship has been destroyed by parenthood. For us, it was the opposite. After the birth of our two children, she doubled down on her efforts to seduce me, to please me, to ensure we had quality time together. I've seen so many women allow their new role as mother to take over, to the point that they forget they are also wives. My wife never neglected me. I remained her favorite. Our love remained her priority. I know that our relationship is a citadel that she will defend no matter what.

I am lucky to have her by my side, I'm aware of that. I fell in love with her at first sight. My wife is sublime— she is almost absurdly beautiful, a beauty that has been chipped away at over time only by her lack of self-confidence. It was clear right away that she wasn't from my world, but that wasn't important: she was different, complicated, complex.

Sometimes, when I go too far, I'm afraid that she'll leave me. The thought makes me dizzy: I don't ever want her to pull away. I want to keep my wife close to me. Sometimes, when she spends a while downstairs, when I call her from upstairs and she doesn't answer, I'm afraid that I'll go down and find that she's hanged herself in the kitchen, or that she's packed her bags and left. I play with the limits, I play with her limits—but I know where they are.

I can't imagine my life without her. This dawned on me a few months after we first met, when she went back to her ex for two weeks. I knew that they had gone to the seaside. I did nothing; I didn't call her, I didn't beg her to come back. But I made myself a promise: if she comes back, I will marry her and build a life with her. She came back and I kept my promise.

On our wedding day, I was happy, but lucid: I knew what I was getting myself into. That day, I wrote vows for her, too, a long letter that I didn't dare read in front of our guests—too modest, I suppose. I know that caused her a lot of pain. But as I often do when she's suffering, I diverted my gaze and waited for it to pass. It's not my fault that she feels everything so intensely, that small irritations cause her such great pain. I can't dry all her tears: that's not my role. My wife isn't looking for a shoulder to cry on, she's looking for a *soulmate* to set her aflame. That's how our relationship functions. After fifteen years together, there is still passion, desire: that's more than most married couples can say.

Make no mistake. By acting this way, I give her what she needs. I fuel her passion for the good of our family. I know her by heart: if we'd had a peaceful relationship, she would have quickly grown bored—and she would have ended up leaving me for a supposedly *great love*. Her romantic engine runs on strong sensations, so I try to maintain a certain cadence. My wife can't go long without a spark.

No notebook or codified system for me, I leave that to my wife. I act on my whims—I do what I like. I go to her when I miss her, and distance myself when she irritates me. Knowing that she's prepared to do anything for me is a comfortable position to be in. Comforting, too, and above all, reassuring. No other woman will ever love me like she does. She's Ariane. She's my wife.

ACKNOWLEDGMENTS

To Sylvie Gracia, my editor, who found my manuscript in the slush pile. Thank you for helping it grow with frankness, rigor, and levity.

To Sophie de Sivry, who believed in my book and bet on it.

To Constance Beccaria, Adèle Leproux, Lise Chaton, Alina Gurdiel, Sophie Langlais, and the entire team at L'Iconoclaste, a wonderful place to write and to visit. A publishing house that's also a home.

To my amazing American editor Gretchen Schmid at HarperCollins: thank you for seeing how *Mon mari* could become *My Husband*—and find its way to the American readers. I learned a lot from you.

To my incredibly talented translator Emma Ramadan: you came into my world and made it speak English. It is what all writers dream of.

ACKNOWLEDGMENTS

To all my readers, at different stages of writing—from my first attempts to the manuscript that I submitted to publishers with my heart racing. You each left an imprint on my book.

To my parents, who have regularly transformed their house into a writing residency for me, to Damien, Marie Lou, and Léonard, to Louise—this family that has always enveloped me with love. I am the luckiest to have you in my life.

To my friends who give me all my strength: Zoé, Lucie, Nicolas, Valentin, Thomas, Maud, Éléonore, Charlotte, Clémence, Marianne, Jeanne, Claudia. You are my secret weapons.

To Pierre, for the joy and the new horizons.

To Marion, my friend and literary guide in the shadows, who showed me the sound of the Breton waves, and without whom this book would not be the same: your perspective on this text and on my life is infinitely precious.

To Michael, who supported me for the three years I was writing this book. I loved you madly.

Maud Ventura lives in Paris. She led the podcast division of one of France's major radio stations and speaks fluent English. *My Husband*, her first novel, is an international bestseller and winner of France's First Novel Prize, the Prix du Premier Roman.

Emma Ramadan (translator) is the recipient of the PEN Translation Prize, the Albertine Prize, an NEA Fellowship and a Fulbright Scholarship. She lives in Brooklyn.